T3-BOE-995

NEW DIRECTIONS 22

N D

New Directions in Prose and Poetry 22

Edited by J. Laughlin

A New Directions Book

Library of Congress Catalog Card Number: 37-1751 (Serial)

ACKNOWLEDGMENTS

Grateful acknowledgment is made to the editors and publishers of books and magazines where some of the selections in this book first appeared: for Gottfried Benn, *Die Stimme hinter dem Vorhang*, Limes Verlag, Wiesbaden, Germany; for James B. Hall, *The Virginia Quarterly Review;* for Richard Meyers, *Don Quixote, Genesis: Grasp, Sanskaras, Works;* for Stuart Montgomery, *Poetry*, Copyright © 1967 by Modern Poetry Association; for Ed Roberson, *The Atlantic, May We Speak*, edited by Gerry Rhodes; for Al Young, *Aldebaran Review, Camels Coming, Perspectives.*

Manufactured in the United States of America
Published simultaneously in Canada by McClelland & Stewart, Ltd.

New Directions Books are published for James Laughlin
by New Directions Publishing Corporation,
333 Sixth Avenue, New York 10014.

CONTENTS

NEW DIRECTIONS 22

GOD CARES, BUT WAITS

JAMES B. HALL

I. *Behind Our Lines*

First the prisoner and his interrogation. Of my final mission into their territory, more later.

Beyond our village the highway crosses a narrow bridge of concrete, and then in a gorge of stone goes north. At four o'clock the subject came pedaling beneath the row of palm trees; I stepped from behind the abutment and grabbed his handle bars. When asked did he "want a drink of our water," the prisoner's face turned white: I had taken another courier headed north.

Our procedures of Search and Interrogation are prescribed: with the subject facing a wall, legs apart, we search first for the knives or other weapons of offense. Only then may we place our hands first on the crown of their heads, rumpling well the hair, then on the seams of clothing where the saw blades are, then down to the shoes—in his case, rope sandals. Inspection of the body cavities, especially females who wear pads or tampons, takes place at my private office in the abandoned schoolhouse. Only after complete inspection may interrogation begin.

Subject courier carried no weapons of offense, but when I placed my hands on the crown of his head I noted a soft innocent odor, a coconut oil pomade. His trousers had neither seams nor fly. When I removed the cycling clips from his ankles, the trousers came apart and exposed completely the lower part of his legs. His "trousers" were only a single piece of cloth, gathered at the waist; the legs were formed very cleverly by use of steel clips. Not until my second interrogation, however, did I see the absolute symmetry of his whole body.

Looking back on that instant of capture, I now wish the prisoner had tried to run. As a C.I. Captain, long in the field, I do not miss; as it was, the subject prisoner pushed his bicycle toward my detachment headquarters. The other natives smiled at me pleasantly —a kind of salute; they knew this was planned at Babe Ruth, and besides, my previous two hundred and seventeen captures are a matter of informal record in the village. That night the prisoner's interrogation began.

But first a word about my methods. In addition to obtaining military secrets and/or agent-contacts in the Territories, I also take unofficial information for my private files: if subject is married, then admitted infidelities; if single, then deviant sexual practice, relations with Self, and all "chance" encounters. These personal notes I send into the village for "secret" typing and reproduction. In this way I am an indirect moral force in the community.

"You are by profession a *Siziar*"—one who professionally washes the dead.

Subject prisoner declined reply.

I then methodically disclosed other items of his file from Babe Ruth. Our files from Corps Headquarters are very complete and contain, chronologically, all instances of unconscious confession as well as the implications from household wastes; at Babe Ruth our specialists analyze evidence from the field for patterns of conduct and consistent routes of travel.

"Your profession and one living relative—your grandmother—are your excuse to go north. Sixty-eight per cent of the time you go via the bridge—at four o'clock."

Subject prisoner declined reply. I then came back to a phrase he had heard before because I had carefully planted it in his subconscious: "How would you like to drink our water?"

Concerning our water this much should be clearly understood. Although the *Rossiter* or the "Lawyer" may be delegated for morale purposes to the enlisted men, including my detachment barber, I alone—in private—administer all water. One half gallon in each nostril is often enough. The head fills, rationality departs, and by delicate adjustments the subject is suspended for some hours in a twilight state of full confession. When professionally administered, fatalities are almost unheard of. At that moment the prisoner remained suspiciously calm and so I put my question once again . . . "the water?"

As though to reply, as though to begin his interrogation of *me* —a Captain six years in rank—my subject reached down and took a cycling clip from his right ankle. The cloth fell away from his leg, and the light turned his thigh to silver.

Without hesitation, I did the only responsible thing. I kneeled before him, and I forcibly *replaced* the cycle clip around his ankle. Then I rang for my orderly. Instead of suggesting the prisoner might wish to "Talk with a Lawyer," I ordered this subject held under special guards, in a stone cell in our stone outbuildings. I now felt this particular prisoner might be a rewarding exercise, after all.

The next morning, I sent my entire C.I. Detachment, including the barber, into the field for ten days. I wished to complete this interrogation under Ideal Conditions. When I asked him again if he wanted a drink of our water, the prisoner looked directly into my eyes, but everywhere in his face I saw genetic weakness. At that time I disclosed, completely, the secondary information in his file: he had washed the young girl overly long. Why? Consider those unhealthy relations with Self. Why? The light behind my desk shone full into his eyes.

My prisoner did not either reply or change expression. Instead, he bent gracefully and removed both cycle clips from his ankles. It was the flesh of his thigh that glistened and winked and moved like liquid metal in the folds of cloth. For the first time I saw the symmetry of his whole body.

As a matter of command decision, I opened my interrogation drawer. On my desk, I placed a bamboo rod, one end flayed. To my surprise the prisoner neither asked for mercy nor made assertions contrary to our cross-filed data from Babe Ruth. Instead, he took the rod from my desk and somewhat awkwardly—like a girl trying to throw a baseball—flayed the sunlight.

"No. Like this," I said, and brought the "C.I. Lawyer" down across my own leg. The prisoner's face was ecstatic. Once he saw our correct methods, he went around and around my private office, striking desk and chairs and the plaster walls.

Only after I removed my own shirt and placed myself on the interrogation bench did he see the obligations of continuity. He, himself, cried out as he brought the bamboo "Lawyer" across my flesh. As I had known he would, the prisoner broke down and began to weep. So ended my second interrogation.

Such was the pattern of our next four days: early each morning I suggested our water; in response, the subject removed his cycle clips. Each day I placed a new mode of investigation on the desk; avidly, he learned our methods. In order, I submitted myself to the knout, the *Rossiter,* the Penis Key, and the Fire Stubbs. Toward the end I even dreamed of the prisoner, head down beside our carboys, a nostril hose swinging in the sunlight like a vine. Still, I held back, and so it was, at night, our bodies exhausted, that we began to talk.

"You have told me of your past," he said. "You came from an outlying Province, and because your father was a Tax-Fraud Investigator, your parents often moved. Only your mother is now alive."

On those nights I disclosed even the secondary information about my childhood: all our white cottages behind picket fences in a hundred villages; helping mother pack china in the barrel of straw for still another move; the ways I kept my teachers morally strong by the little notes addressed to the superintendents of all my old school districts. . . .

As though it were his voice speaking, I heard about my interesting past: recruit days, my medals for services in the Territories as Chief of Patrol; my sought-for commission, and my satisfactory advance to Captain, Counter Insurgency. Sometimes his hand lay on my breast and in the darkness of my room we were prisoner and interrogator, almost intimate, almost One. Very much I wanted to administer our water, but this he denied me in the following way.

"Captain," he said on the final night, taking care to speak with appropriate respect. "I will now do the thing within my power." He raised me by the hand, and I followed to a room where already he had laid out the ritualistic towels of a *Siziar.*

His insistent hands bathed and bathed me until at three o'clock the telephone beside my bed—my direct line to Babe Ruth—began to ring.

The voice on the wire was Tiger, at Babe Ruth. In code, our Operations Major gave me the co-ordinates of a new transmitter —deep in the Territories to the north. At once I volunteered for this mission. Tiger denied my request. I remonstrated. At last he sensed the urgency in my voice and he agreed I should draw grenades at Dump Two. In less than thirty minutes, crepe-soled scouting sandals on my feet, my body covered by a native burnoose, I began my last patrol.

Subject prisoner wept without restraint at my departure. Only once did I look back: from the door of the abandoned schoolhouse, his back to the light, he was watching me go. When I returned he would be gone, for as a token I had given him my private key to his outbuilding cell. Under formal orders once more, I walked steadily across the valley. At dawn I drew grenades from a watchman at Dump Two, and then crossed easily into their Territories to the north.

On the second day, high in the mountains, I crawled beneath bushes and came to the barbed wire surrounding their transmitter. This place was of hard, swept clay, the red and white tower clean and erect in the open space beyond the fence. Beside the tower I saw a house of cinder blocks, with a low, square, green door. Pacing the strict limits of his post, a very large man—a guard—sometimes shouted cadence to himself as he walked. With grenades and the machine pistol held close to my belly, I covered myself with my leaf-colored burnoose and waited for dusk.

Shortly past noon I saw the relief guard arrive on the back seat of a motorcycle. To be far behind the lines and to see them talking in their green uniforms and arm bands is always sinister. This new guard was slender, and obviously less military. At once the new guard went into the transmitter house and in the quiet of the afternoon I heard the noise of a toilet flushing.

Finally the new guard returned to the post—with a folded beach chair. The guard leaned the rifle beside the door and unfolded the chair. With the motorcycle now far away, the guard removed first hat, and then blouse. After an almost knowing look around the perimeter fence, the guard took off her brassiere. She reclined in her chair, her face to the sun, her red hair winking in the light.

This new guard—a woman—apparently drifted off into sun-bathed sleep.

All afternoon, through a little opening in the briers, I watched the woman "guard" their transmitter. Clearly she was my enemy and yet from time to time she roused herself and peered very innocently, yet very intently, into the hand mirror in her purse. Always before on my patrols I had used explosives, guile, disguise, appeals to pride, or bribery where possible. Now, for reasons I did not understand, I felt beyond Tiger and even Corps; in fact, although I still say our war is Just, I felt beyond the entire chain of our command, both tactically and politically. I began to tremble in my burnoose, and yet with grenades and automatic pistol warm near my belly, I forced myself to wait.

What happens next is perhaps strange: some will say I wanted to die, but the fact of my victory proves otherwise. Boldly at dusk, I stood up. I went directly to the main gate: she did not challenge. Therefore I went to the place where she lay. At close range she was much younger than I had imagined. Provocatively—innocently—in the half light from the transmitter tubes, I saw her teeth and her half-parted lips. For one moment, pistol at full automatic, I stood above her.

Suddenly her eyes opened. Without trying to rise she spoke to me in my mother tongue and she said, "You have come."

In fury I remembered Corps and Tiger. I armed and then I threw my first grenade. I threw it with great force inside the transmitter. Only then did she cry out. Too late, she saw my face bent very close above her lips.

She cried out again, but I threw my last grenades into the now flaming house. Suddenly, I heard laughter. This was my own voice. As I ran across the clearing and leaped the fence and ran down a ravine of stones, I heard the transmitter tower crash down into the clearing somewhere behind me.

I repeat: although the woman guard awoke and positively identified my face, I did not shoot.

On the trails through low jungle to the south, I sometimes wept. Too late I saw that my prisoner—now escaped—and the woman guard were in league: what the prisoner began, the woman finished. And it was a fact: I had spared them both.

Therefore imagine my intense joy when I arrived back at the

village and crossed the narrow concrete bridge. I found the schoolhouse still abandoned—except for my prisoner. He had remained faithful. He had even prepared for my return, for food was already on the table. At once I slipped out of my burnoose and my sandals and together we ate.

From gratitude and from some apparently deeper understanding, I very willingly taught my prisoner—at last—to administer the water. His confession was lyrical, complete.

Awkwardly at first, then with greater control, he administered the same to me. One half gallon in each nostril is often enough.

Painfully at first, then in a visionary way, all consciousness left—and then returned. In the end, my body outraged by water, I sank again into the isolated darkness of the abandoned schoolhouse. Toward dawn, I very clearly heard the prisoner going through the drawers of my interrogation desk, taking one of each thing I had taught him—correctly—to use.

Unable to arise, impotent, my Detachment still in the field, I heard the back door slam. The prisoner, after all, was going north. Somewhere this side of the mountain he would meet the woman guard. They would cross-file their notes and together they would view all of the things he had taken from my interrogation desk; together they would go to some house I would never see and there, late at night, they would make their full report. As for myself, I knew well enough what both my sergeant and the barber would report to Tiger and also to Babe Ruth.

Not far up the gorge of stone I heard men counting cadence lustily as they came. I heard my own Detachment march across the narrow concrete bridge and then up the path toward this abandoned schoolhouse.

II. *Outside the Cave*

The buildings of the city and of the prison itself were fire under the sky and the land beyond the city's edge with no rain in the past two years was cracked as an old woman's hand: cattle with legs apart in the fence corners, mouths slobbering foam, eyes glazed by the memory of water. In that heat he passed walls of stucco where the noise of buckets swinging empty above empty cisterns echoed among the small shops that lay beside the railroad tracks going north across the valley until the rails became a sliver of steel between two hills and then went on into the Territories beyond. To himself he said, "No. Not yet."

"Going on?" the barber asked and with a white paper bib in place the barber began with the clippers. "*Very* far?"

The man said nothing for truly he had no plans. Although he had waited years for his release, and although his papers were correct, he now accepted something for the first time: in a coastal city where they had interrogated and arraigned and had tried him, indeed in the whole world, there was no one waiting for him. Years ago his only sister had stood by him for awhile, but now even the judges were dead.

"Shorter than that," he ordered the barber, and because he was now free, with good papers, his voice was contemptuous.

"Yes indeed, sir," and the barber went on: so this year not one land owner planted a crop. And to be honest about it, in the whole town only one garden remained green. That one, by rail, twice weekly, got barrels of water marked Salt Cod—it was said. Also: young girls roamed the streets after dark, the government did nothing, and so who was to blame?

The man in the barber chair said nothing, but he heard well enough that girls ran alone in the streets after dark. In the sky overhead he felt some grotesque fowl—all fire—beat its wings.

"Good luck," the barber finally said, and with false enthusiasm whipped off the paper bib. Released prisoners often ducked into his shop like this for they wanted to pay someone to do a personal service, perhaps for the first time in years. The barber resolved to say no more for this one was very pale and very hard and very possibly a murderer—or worse. When the ex-convict looked at him coldly the barber added nervously, "Ahhh, good luck. Ahhh out *there*?"

As the prisoner walked along the railroad tracks going north, he happened to look up and see the cave. Because he was going nowhere at all, he climbed the high bank to see about it. This cave was in a ledge of rock and not much larger than his old cell. Inside the cave there was nothing at all; outside the cave's entrance was a large, smooth square of clay.

Because he was fatigued, the convict sat for a while on the

square of earth to rest. Toward the town at dusk he saw the lights of the prison workshops suddenly blaze in the heat; along the tracks to the north he saw only the landscape and the rampant heat of the valley flow across the hills like a river.

With no possessions except for the suit of blue serge and the small amount of money they had paid him for work at the stamping machines in the prison, with no very real hope of a future, the convict saw no reason to move on. The money left over from the barbershop was not enough for either bribery or a train ticket; therefore he threw all his coins over the bank toward the railroad tracks. He took off the prison-made suit coat and the shoes and placed them behind a rock in the cave. In the old way, exactly at nine o'clock, he slept.

At daylight the convict sat again in the mouth of his cave. For the first time in his life, without rancor, he observed the sun's first rays come up and then spread across the curve of the earth. On the train tracks below, the first peasant walked toward the white buildings of the town; past noon a released prisoner in a blue serge suit walked north, eyes on the gravel. No one looked up at the cave in the limestone ledge so the ex-convict who had committed so many crimes against both women and animals did not call down. He watched his morning shadow disappear at noon; he watched his afternoon shadow grow longer and disappear at night when the sun went down.

On the third day the ex-convict slept upright, and awoke to find a youth standing on the square of clay before him.

"Are your lips black because of no water?" was what the boy said, for he was an unemployed drover who had found several coins on the clay bank. One after another these coins had led him upward to this cave. Because the convict had been so long in a cell, he had somewhat lost the habit of speech and so he made no reply at all. As a little joke he even pretended not to see the money that the young drover showed him.

From guilt and also from the joy of having found coins that a man in a cave did not claim as his own, the drover boy went at once into the town. At cafés, a little at each place, he spent the money and he recounted also his adventure with a black-lipped hermit. Old women begging at tavern doorways heard this story and each one knew in her heart that if one coin were found there was always another.

At dawn the convict awoke to see a half circle of townspeople staring into his blackened, sun-warped face. A beggarwoman had found the last of his coins on the clay bank above the tracks; in a respectful voice, she gave thanks. The drover boy stepped forward to ask all of their questions: In fact, had The Hermit been without food *or* water for seven months? Did or did not one melon roll down from the bank above the cave each night and thus sustain him? In what manner were certain of the clay-bank coins changed overnight, in merchant's tills, into gold?

The former convict felt laughter deep in his belly. Once he had been a stonemason but much drink and a vicious temper had caused him to kill a fellow workman. The body had floated many days down a canal, and his first crime was not discovered; after that his violence became more open, and there were others. Finally, almost by chance, he was questioned about a woman's body and the child's body dead beside her. At the trial other things were established. To hear their deferential questions made him feel superior, much in the way his crimes had made him feel beyond the judgment of all men. In addition, he saw one of these "pilgrims" was a young girl with black, serious hair down around her shoulders. The old echoes of desire clanged and clanged in his mind but because he had worked as a mason he thought, "Let's first see how this little job goes. . . ."

With all of the guile and dissimulation he had learned in prison, the convict solemnly raised his right hand, palm outward toward their faces. Well enough he saw the young woman was frightened: this was good for he knew from experience that genuine fright may easily become passion.

As protection against the dust, one man had cloth over his face and so the convict did not at once recognize the barber. As though on official business, the barber walked slowly around the convict: very closely the barber inspected the half-moons of scalp above the ears, the slope of the forehead, the gray-tippd hair growing wildly from each nostril.

"Of course I would know the prisoner by his neck and his hair. Besides, I never forget a customer who tips generously. This man is not the man who came into my shop. I give you my word, this hair was not recently trimmed by a fine barber such as myself."

The first delegation from the town walked back along the railroad tracks and the beggarwomen followed, making little pods of dust with their sticks, looking for more coins.

The convict watched them go and then rolled backward into his cave and laughed until tears came into his eyes. He felt these people were even bigger fools than either wardens or prison guards, themselves always prisoners but because of the pay never admitting it. Nevertheless, to keep up appearances, the prisoner sat again outside his cave and was surprised to see that one visitor—beyond any doubt the barber—had donated a few coins. This new money the convict also threw over the bank: others would find it when the sun rose the following day.

Then it began. Beggars and the small shop owners who sold cloth and crushed maize walked out along the railroad tracks. They left melons, gourds of water, or coins; each night the convict threw these coins wildly across the landscape for the people who found the money also spread his fame most swiftly to the larger cities where now all canals were dry.

Because trainloads of people came early and a great many stayed to imitate the convict's peculiar cross-legged posture or to imitate the way he stared at the landscape, the prisoner found he could not easily retreat into his cave either to laugh or to take a long, secret drink of gourd water. He saw new respect in their faces, and this he had not known as either a prisoner or an honest but violent stonemason; he felt he deserved this attention for none of his trials had been covered well enough by the Press.

Unfortunately, their gifts and coins were in such profusion around his crossed legs that he could scarcely move. This effect of opulence distracted his pilgrims from closely inspecting his almost black body and neck and face. In the past week the barber had closed his shop and was now living at the foot of the clay bank beside the tracks. In his loud warden's voice the barber lectured each day's crowds and told them what to expect when they climbed the bank, and also of the miracles: Copper into Gold, and the Profusion of Melons.

Partly to offset these distractions, on the ninety-sixth day the convict, who now really did look much like a hermit, motioned for the young girl to remain beside him for the night. Each day, without fail, she had walked to his cave and he understood she wanted to experience his body for herself.

"Do . . ." and he was surprised at his own voice for he had imagined his first words to her as sounding not coarse, "This, do . . ." and he picked up one coin from the heap and managed to toss it almost to the railroad tracks.

The young girl did likewise. He saw she liked very much to throw the gifts and the melons down upon the barber who suddenly found himself kneeling under a shower of coins.

Desire was what the convict felt, desire clanging in his blood. His hands ached as he thought of the white throat of the girl and of twisting fiercely her black hair around her throat until at the same instant he both defiled her and broke the neck with his remembering, stonemason hands.

"Place me inside our cave," he said. "Pour all water gourds over my unclothed body."

This the girl did, and then without having to be asked she threw herself on his breast and sobbed, "Yes . . . Yes."

Ironically, the convict now knew his lust was only in his mind. His gulps of water late at night when the barber slept, his fast, the sun all day and the dust, all those things had wasted his body to . . . oh, to these crossed sticks that were his legs, to these bones that were his thighs, to a protruding, black forehead, to flesh that now seemed almost stone.

She wanted to revive his flesh, but she could only weep in the cave. In his pretension he could only say to her, "Believe, believe." Then he, himself, was taken by her innocent, smooth-handed desire. To her, yes; but to himself nothing happened.

"But we could," the girl told him softly as she carried him once more to his customary place at the entrance of his cave. "If you will only permit rain to fall. In the valley."

Partly to please her, partly to fulfill the role he had drifted into over the months, partly to perpetuate this joke on the herd-minded bourgeois that he so much despised, but most of all for revenge, the convict said it solemnly, one eye on her white throat:

"Rain," he said to the dry moonlight. It was the kind of joke another convict might understand. "Rain. *Comes.*"

After the girl called those words down over the railroad bank, the convict saw the barber running along the tracks toward the town, already making manifest this promised miracle.

Yet in the days that followed, the heat overhead beat the entrance of the cave with wings of fire. Now he wore no clothes at all; bleached by the sun, his hair waved across his rutted breast. In his mind he saw what he had become: a thing of influence, his words recorded by the friends of the barber. To men who left much gold where he could see it, the convict passed on a convict's evasive, worldly wisdom; these men of substance used his words to justify business schemes that were both devious and cruel. For this service they left water he could not now drink in gourds of gold.

For two weeks, with longing, he watched the smoke plumes and fire of the railroad trains going across the valley toward the lighted cities on the coast. He thought upon it seriously: he would take only the coins of gold and he would bribe the drover boy to sit in his place for one night. Secretly he would leave this cave and board the train and disappear forever. Yet at summer's end the convict saw it was already too late. And of course he knew: to excuse his own weakness and also to perpetuate the lie of his apparent renunciation of her flesh, impotent and wan, in a moment of sentimentality he had spoken two words and now those words were his ultimate act of deception; to insure the illusion of both simple folk and the prosperous fools, to focus attention on himself, he had promised rain. He felt entangled in the hopeless vines of his own promise. His own words had reduced him to this sack of flesh. His condition was testimony to his own inflexibility and to his own vision of fraud. His days and his nights became one. This was his end.

Oh, he was dying. This comprehension came as both shadow and sunlight when the great wings of heat beat upward without remorse against the cloudless cave of the sky overhead. No rain came and in the delusion of all light the echoes faded inside the cave. Near the end he heard only the monotone of his own blood making the noise of a freight train dying somewhere inside this solitary cell of flesh that was once a man.

For the past week the girl had slept beside him, waiting for the end.

In the final hour when he was beyond movement of either lip or hand, he felt a moment of consciousness spring up like the last flame on a hearth place. In that instant he heard a distant sound. He heard it once again. He heard the thunder stamping, heard noise splinter the sky.

He opened his eyes. He saw the girl standing in the cave's mouth, arms upspread, legs apart. In the sky beyond her legs, he saw the great slave whips of lightning lacerate both the clouds and the earth. He heard it clearly, heard it across the valley, heard the thousand feet of a running cloudburst: the rain, the . . . r . . . ain.

Half-believing, for a second believing absolutely in himself after all, he knew he was dead, dead and running down the clay bank and across the railroad tracks, running through the downpour into the valley beyond, submitting himself at last to the formal resignation of all landscape.

III. *A Transfiguration by Vines*

They awoke in a small valley, a gorge of stones leading down into the town. Beyond the guardrails overhead they heard first an automobile and then two carts on the blacktop road going down; behind and high above on the mountain where once they had camped, they heard the noise of woodchoppers at work in the fir trees. The man raised his head. Beneath the guardrails, as always, he saw the road curving away, to reappear at last near a fountain in a green park and go on then into the town below.

The woman turned on her side of their blankets. By raising her head she could also view the place where they sometimes felt they wanted very much to go—at least after long discussions they had agreed once on that point. Now it seemed mostly a matter of time, and the time was not yet.

"Fires," and she tried to take exactly her share of their blankets. Because she was domestic and responsible and hungry she said, "Other women—down there—are at breakfast."

The man took it as a criticism, but did not reply. He was more philosophical and he often thought back to see how it had all begun —so to speak. For a few minutes he looked at the gorge where tiers of young fir trees rose above them, sparkling with moisture in these first minutes of another day. Higher up on the mountain the woodchoppers worked steadily in the larger trees.

He threw back his side of the blanket: the vine was still there. He had known it would not go away during the night, but its new growth each day was always shocking. Nevertheless, he was always anxious to see how much it really had grown during the night while they slept.

Yes. This morning really a great deal—as he pointed out to her. Whether this growth was caused by these longer, late-summer days, or by the night's humidity, he could not say. At first he had thought the vine's growth was in relationship to phases of the moon; now he was equally convinced that new growth was related to the water level in the trout stream in the bottom of the gorge. Water, from somewhere, must surely give the vine both food and useful minerals in solution; otherwise, how would the green convoluting vine with its leaves like hammered green metal, tendrils soft as his wife's flesh, continue to grow?

Actually, they had come here in late spring. They had walked down a trail from the melting end of the mountain glacier. When lights of the town seemed very close they had camped in this spot below the guardrails for the night.

The vine, so tiny then, had been there when they awoke. She had intended to throw back their blanket, but he was already sitting upright, examining very intently this small green thing, the first leaf emergent and tender and silly there between his great toe and his second toe. He had said, "Fungus," but as they both watched, a new tendril curled up and out, and by nine o'clock this first new, green leaf was a little bit larger.

"What about stockings?" she had asked, for it was still a few miles to the town, or at least to the green park where the fountain was.

He might have said, "No," or he might have argued that this, too, was a living thing, but he did not; instead, he accepted it without either fear or discussion. He saw it was without roots and loved the sun and that seemed enough; therefore, they stopped all activity and all future plans in order to contemplate this new, tiny thing that was even then growing larger from between his toes.

Some days he lay with his head on the rucksack, and she lay beside him, and both of them watched his foot and the vine growing. At noon she went to the trout stream and brought back small cups of water to pour over his foot—and also to inspect more closely this new thing that was now really much larger and much more beautiful. Then past noon, when the woodcutters stopped chopping, they slept.

Toward nightfall they awoke and she took a little of their food from the rucksack and they ate together. Even after they went to sleep again beneath the stars they felt the vine's newest tendril rustle a little around his ankle and—later—around the calf of his leg. Even in the nights of late summer they did not dream and at dawn they contemplated his new green leg, made green by the vine growing.

At the end of their second month, she realized the vine itself had become his life. This she accepted. His single-minded attention, his hard-minded exclusion of everything else, in fact his adoration of the vine, instead of either her, or their own relationship, made her feel lonely. Once she cried in the night, but he did not awaken. The bad, blue feeling came and she, herself, wished for the green vine to grow inside her belly. But no, and that mood also passed.

Nevertheless, during that night, she recalled a great deal about their old life before this vine came to them: at a place, a town it was in the Territories to the north. They had met when young. What it was like before they met, she did not now care to remember. At first they had gone out at night with other young people in groups; later, alone, they had experimented with drugs and went for long, harmless trips of the "mind"—singly, of course—but still much closer than ever before.

Finally when they were truly together, they had gone into the mountains toward the foot of the glacier. For several days they had camped near beds of wild flowers in bloom—of that much she was certain. Now each day the vine grew a little bit—like a habit—and now it held them both. She did not cry about this anymore and when the tendrils of the vine took his thigh, when she could no longer see all of his body in the old way, she accepted it.

Acceptance, however, was not enough. At times he urged her to leave him, to go on alone into the town. She felt this was neither ultimate affection, nor even mercy on his part for now the roots of the vine had pierced through the blankets and went deeply into the rocks and the soil. If he urged her to leave, it was his way of being a hero; besides, he would have the vine alone and unadulterated for himself. That he could tell her to go on alone made her sad. After all, she had carried all of the water from the trout stream. She had accommodated the vine in their bed from the first day it appeared—innocent and tender—between his toes.

In September, before the rains, the thing finally happened. Deeply, she had wanted it to happen: she awoke but could not get up to serve either him or his vine. During the night, because she had always placed her legs close to his in sleep, the tendrils of the vine had taken her ankles. As they watched, the tendrils ravished her flesh and took her strength as though the vine needed this new thing on which to grow.

When the first rains of fall came down the gorge they did not move for they were both with this vine and—at last—a part of it.

At noon she felt him tremble beside her. What she saw was the first spume of snow, blowing down from the glacier and across the upper rim of the gorge. His breath at noon emerged from his part of the leaves, and she saw his breath turn white against the vine. Worse, the vine itself was now, ever so little, turning to brown.

In fear, in panic, with their rusted camp knife, he began to hack at the vine. When the vine drew back, she saw his neck and his breast. When she saw him again, for the first time in many months, she too began to pull and to cut each tendril frantically. Then each of them got a knife and the vine seemed to pull back and away—but not one tendril withered.

Still, she urged him on. Together they worked at each tendril in order; beginning at the top they pried tendrils from flesh, and did not stop when blood came from each place where the vine had to let go. That night, very late, the first flakes of snow fell in their camp and the vine was almost gone from their bodies.

"Tomorrow," he told her, and she too felt they were free to go. "Tomorrow we will go down into the town."

To her it seemed only an act of the Will, and so she put everything she could reach into small piles. Very early in the old way they would get up and pack and go on down the road which they had seen each day all summer. Oh, she knew they were exhausted but she knew they were also together in the old way, in the time before they watched this thing which they had nurtured and had finally accepted and which had, in the end, almost overwhelmed them both. "Good."

And then she added, "I still do." And he answered her and said, "Yes. I still do. I love you."

And then it was morning.

During the night the vine had surrounded them, had grown back tighter than ever before. Now they could not see each other.

Because snow was coming down the side of the mountain very fast, the woodcutters—two of them—doubled-bitted axes over their shoulders, also came down the trails to the road.

That morning the two woodcutters saw this strange thing not far from the guardrails: a vine growing, with great roots going down into the soil. Furthermore, the vine had grown in upon itself—had not climbed either the guardrail or a tree, nor had it run across the rocks of the gorge toward the water, as might be thought natural. More strange than its shape was this: the coiling, triumphant vine seemed to breathe in and out. When the woodchoppers placed their woolly ears close to the leaves they heard voices—or something—crying out from the core.

Therefore the woodcutters chopped this very large vine off at its roots. They also chopped away the stray tendrils. With leftover vines they made the whole thing into a long, mummylike bundle. They also cut down a small fir tree and stripped off the branches to make a carrying pole. With the bundle of vine tied to the pole, they placed the pole on their shoulders. With axes and pole and all they went down the road and around the curves. Whistling as they walked along, the woodcutters soon entered an astonished village.

In that way, riding on a pole, intimate in vines, concealed from the people who watched with much interest as they passed, the man and the woman came to the place which they had looked at from afar for a very long time.

In the town square all of the following week the children and beggarwomen and men going home from barbershops or factories on the hill and home from prison or from some army post not far from the frontiers, all of them walked past, and some of them paused for a little while to look. More than one said, "Yes. Something is singing all right, somewhere inside those wrapped-up vines."

And then they walked on.

THE ENIGMA OF HO CHI MINH'S FUNERAL

LAWRENCE FERLINGHETTI

I am walking down the middle
of Telegraph Avenue Berkeley
in the middle of the surrealist riddle
which is Ho Chi Minh's funeral
Revolution
comes out a thirdstorywindow
on a recordplayer
Whatever
colors the mind
is a raga
Red Ganges
washes over mine
as water over shallows
When the mode of the music changes
someone throws bathwater out
with a burning baby in it
The people's parade
makes a U-turn
and washes up at the door
of the Free Church
where they hang up Ho's portrait
with red&black flags on the Cross

They are passing out red&green flowers
and reading Ho Chi Minh's Prison Poems
from the pulpit
An old friend I never knew very well
comes up & kisses me
waving her new black baby
A black tank trundles by waving its red light
and whining electronically
Back in Genoa Street
Nadja opens the door of her womb
to Philip Lamantia
It is illuminated by a very small lightbulb
neither black nor red
I stand there reading
a counter-revolutionary poem by Yevtushenko
which claims truth is no longer truth
when the Revolution incidentally
sets fire to a loved one's roof
At the corner of Grant & Filbert
another Nadja named Natasha Nevsky
comes to bid me a red-eyed goodbye
on her way to a bed
in the hometown of Dostoevsky
I join the parade again
in my red Volkswagen tepee
A very small party of poets joins me
The photo of Ho seems to be saying ho-ho
hollowly
Waving a small black flag
which turns red subsequently
I run over my family
Accidently

MOURNER'S KADDISH

MARK JAY MIRSKY

> *Magnified and sanctified be His great name in the world which He has created according to His will. May He establish His kingdom during your life and during your days and during the life of all the house of Israel, even speedily and at a near time, and say you, Amen.*
>
> *—Hebrew Prayer Book*

The hand lay like a corpse on the table. It was a gnarled claw, wasted to the bones in a fist as tight as *rigor mortis.* It lay still on the rickety oak table, the flat ribbons of the veins so close to the skin that it seemed as if the flesh had been washed away by time and its blood dried blue and purple on the bone.

Nothing was in its grip. It did not stir an inch.

Across the wooden surface, facing the clenched, unmoving hand, a long ragged fingernail at the end of a gigantic finger scratched back and forth on the splinters of oak.

At the top of the table, four nimble fingers, pale white, wrinkled, drummed and drummed, occasionally twitching sideways with arthritis.

At the very end of the table, opposite the four dancing joints, a fat thumb rocked peacefully.

"A Shandeh!" cried Rappowitz as his corpse of a hand leaped into the air, the emaciated fist bursting into fingers, four curling nails clawing the air.

For a few seconds the hand beat alone. Dust and its soft fall were heard in the room. Dust was thick as earth in the reading room of the old Orthodox Synagogue. Bright sunshine pouring through the windows of the ancient chamber grew spotted and faded; its rays fell sluggishly through the room; darkening, they nodded sleepily, slowly meandering, flecks, floating to the floor, illuminating a nose, an ear, a finger, in the late afternoon.

All that room, even the stale air, slept in the dust. As if one of Job's shards had been shattered over all, dry dung descended. Dust mantled the shoulders of the four figures, its soft fall.

Listen! The breath of Chomollofsky the giant returns. His wind scrapes the hoarse bellows in his throat. Muzzel's drunken snore, half a sigh, half a song, sings against the window in an echo. One of the four fingers of Tsinger taps on the board, snaps in the air, and at last the actor cries, "A Shandeh and a Charpeh!"

The four figures stirred. It was a cue.

The five curling fingers in the air froze. They gripped an imaginary thing. "Shkootz!" shrieked Rappowitz. And he hurled it from his hand. He hurled it with the one-time force of Chomollofsky. It burst from his palm with the power of David's sling, spun through the chamber, smashed the window, going right through the hole, and flying across the street shattered the foreheads of Shkootzim all over Roxbury. Shkootzim black and white lay dead on the pavements and the Police had to cart them away by the hundreds. One stone! One stone!

And that stone lay on the floor right under Rappowitz's nose. The stone that had come through the identical hole in the window, ten minutes ago. A stone that had the nerve to fly into a holy chamber and bruise the cheek of the giant Chomollofsky, which had never in its eighty years endured such a thing. A stone thrown in the sacred hours of the Shalosh Sudoth!

The stone issued forth out of a group of screaming children, one or two white faces but mostly black. It had come through a window washed by the green waves of time, worn thin as a cheap crystal, stained in a yellowing hue. The stone put its fist through the glass and tore a path through the ghostly flesh of Chomollofsky's huge cheek. The old men stared at the drops of blood that oozed like tears slowly shedding from the wound.

"Police! Police!" screamed Rappowitz through the hole at the mob of excited, youthful, black demons. Laughter shook a few more shreds of glass from the sieved pane as the children leaped up and down. The Police were a thousand blocks away. The Police had sworn never to come near the neighborhood again. The Police were further away than they had been in the last pogrom of Kiev. The Boston Police made an oath in blood never to come into that part of Dorchester forever.

So it was a miracle. A siren out of nowhere. Right on the last foolish shout, "Police!" It scattered the gang with enough rocks in their hands to stone all to death. Like a handful of pebbles the sound flung children from block to block, scattering before it. Yet the old men didn't even look through the hole to see the ambulance go by. They stared at the giant Chomollofsky's cheek.

It made them sick. Blood! Blood! A plague of Egypt.

Blood now bloomed on the white cheek of Chomollofsky as if he were being slaughtered for the First Born. From the depths of his seven-foot frame, more blood had bubbled up than the doctors at Beth Israel could have suspected. A pint washed away under the table before the silk bandage of a threadbare prayer shawl clotted the cut. The blood ran its fingers down the length of the shawl and caked in the bunched folds against his cheek.

With his free hand, Chomollofsky waved Tsinger back to his seat. He didn't want an ambulance for a cut, a nick. He didn't want the butchers from City Hospital or the bills from Beth Israel. He didn't want a cubicle at the Hebrew Home for the Aged. He wanted to sit at the Shalosh Sudoth and speak as a scholar.

Yet for ten minutes, no one said a word.

It was the Shalosh Sudoth. It was time for ten thousand words. It was time for the deeds of Rabbi Yohan Ben Zakkai, who supported all Israel in his old age, to come and shake the foundations of the Synagogue. It was the hour of Rabbi Akiba, his twenty-four thousand students, and his faithful wife. It was time to talk of clean and unclean, and Rabbi Eleazer, whose opinion the Almighty supported in the Schoolhouse, causing trees to fall, rivers to run backward, the walls to incline, His own voice to trumpet forward, and all to no avail because the other Rabbis were stubborn that day. It was that moment when Talmud was to burst the dam of time and rushing forward, choked with a thousand anecdotes bubbling up and down in the text, stories, jokes, gossip, risqué remarks, carry them off two thousand years to the golden halls of Sepphoris and Nehardea.

Amalek had left them speechless. Amalek was out in the street, that gang of Shvartzas and Goyim. For two and more decades, the Goyim of Codman Square had threatened the Temple Erie Street behind the Synagogue, its Jewish hoodlums, had blocked the way. On a Saturday in the old days, the fists and threats of Erie had been jealous for the honor of the Schul. Not so much as a car came down the street to disturb its prayers. Men of the earth, but their shoulders were the foundation of the Temple.

The pious ignoramuses were removed from the back seats of the Temple. It was appointed that they earn money. Into their hovels, onto their crumbling porches and up their back steps, smelling of garbage, came others. Little dark children began to hang around the Schul doors, coming up to the old men, tugging at their coats and suit jackets. At first they seemed cute. The parents were well behaved. Solomon sings, "black but comely." Our father, Moses, married a Cushite.

These moved on. And another crowd came in behind. With strange caps on their heads—Egyptians? Torn jerseys, filthy pants, lounging all day, up and down the sidewalks. Trouble came with them. Sticks and stones. A knife or a razor. The old Rabbi from Roxbury's Rooshashah Schul walked home one night through the park. Why not? Was it Poland? Was it Germany? A mild man, a scholar, his throat was cut and his body tossed in the bushes.

All around, up to the very sills of the Synagogue windows, was a sea of black faces. The building was deserted. They promoted the Shummus to Rabbi. He was never around though. A minyan was a thing of the past. The street outside was too dangerous to walk.

Four was no magic number. Why did they stay? Here they were nothing.

Anywhere else they were dirt. Dirt! Dirt!

Seven feet of Chomollofsky was bent in two. He was a hospital case. He wasn't the Chomollofsky who had sent peasants twice his weight tumbling into the rivers of Poland, a barge captain who loaded up in Odessa with a fortune of goods and poled up the streams of Russia, drawing a crew behind him till muscles bulged like ship's knots on his arms. He wasn't the Chomollofsky whose name was inscribed on the marble tablets in the hallway as the Synagogue's Treasurer, year after year, giving his money away in America, money that didn't flow back into his pockets each year as the rivers rose. Chomollofsky came over a rich man and stayed to be a pauper. The Community that was supposed to take care of him had disappeared. His name was only on the lips of the tablet in the hallway.

Chomollofsky sat with his face clotted to the prayer shawl toward Tsinger. The giant's long finger scratched the table.

Silence. . . What could the former have said to the latter?

What could you say to Tsinger, the old Song and Dance man who had tapped his way from Vilna to Boston nonstop. Tsinger, the Talmud Chochem of Yiddish Burlesque, whose bones like an ox on the way to the altar were hobbled with arthritis: Tsinger, whose hooves had danced upside down on the curtains across Europe and America; Tsinger was now doing a slow shuffle to the grave.

You could say, "Tsinger, sing to us!" Croon to us in that voice you used to have, when the violins stopped, that little tenor that tingled in the crystal streamers of the chandeliers, till the balconies shed tears and the Theatre filled with light; as Eleazer ben Arak sang of mystical things to his master Yohanan on their journey till fire was drawn down from Heaven and the trees of the field flamed bursting forth into song and rainbows shot across the sky. The yellow leaf of Angels, their wings, beat the air. "Ascend! Ascend!" cried a voice. And all were drawn up to Heaven for a banquet.

"Ashes and blotten. . . ashes and blotten. . ." muttered Chomollofsky, laying the clotted prayer shawl down on the dark table. "Go home to die," he mumbled, trying to pick himself out of the chair. He was too weak. He leaned back to collect his strength. No one had noticed. The creaking seat, however, broke the silence.

"Raba. . ." It was Rappowitz speaking. Rappowitz who had been standing, staring ahead as if the rock he had flung, rebounding, struck him senseless, Rappowitz, now picking his eyes up from the stone on the floor, ". . . Raba said, 'Death, it was no more than the prick of a cupping bowl.' "

The room was absolutely quiet. Along the shelves of the chamber, bowed like ailing spines, decaying musty volumes, fly-spotted refugees from the lost Yeshivas of Europe weighed and pondered the remark in the humus of their pages.

For a moment the boards creaked.

Again, all was still. Bits of parchment and leather crumbled at the edge of books, splintering into the dust of the air, filling the room with decay, its odor. In the great hall next to the reading chamber, there were cobwebs under the seats. Rappowitz knew. He had been in there in the morning. The Rabbi showed up, saw, said, "No minyan," smiled, and walked out. What could you do? It was the law. The ark was full of moldering scrolls. The good ones had been carried away to Newton.

The Synagogue was wealthy. Don't worry! Only the money was in Newton where they had put up another building and there was a waiting list three blocks long to get in. Out there, this morning, the parking lot was filled with Cadillacs and Lincoln Continentals. If they had wanted to, they could have sent a Chrysler station wagon or two, into Dorchester. Israel was full of deceptions. Rappowitz was willing to stretch a point, to overlook. There were supposed to be black Jews in the world. Why didn't they show up?

Oh, Rappowitz had been out to Newton for a look. There was nothing there. It wasn't a House of Study. It was a Community Center, a Rumpus Room, a Country Club, and there was a two thousand dollar initiation fee to get in.

Better to sit in the cobwebs, the Saturday afternoons of the past. The Shalosh Sudoth when he was President! Before the Crash, in the days of his sock factory. He still had the boxes in his house and door to door, he eked out a living selling moth-eaten socks. Rappowitz pushed the socks to the back of his mind. The room was filling up with the past. Orthodox came from all over America to listen in. There were dialecticians who could shame the Rabbis of Pumbeditha with their wit, argument, scholarship. The voices of controversy over a learned point shattered the panes in their frames.

The gold bole of the sun flashed through the hole in the window, stinging his eyes. Now they had only his memory, Chomollofsky rarely spoke, Muzzel snored. . .

The Synagogue in Dorchester couldn't go on much longer. Soon boards would cross the door. For two months there had been no minyans for Shabbos. Three men died, two moved away, and one could no longer come. Tsinger wasn't regular in his attendance. There was no one coming into the neighborhood. Only one sure thing. Rappowitz looked across the room at the rise and fall of a purple nose, Muzzel, whose Yiddish nickname, "Lucky," was borne out by experience. The drunken waddle somehow gave him an immunity from attack. Eighty years old and he outdrank the hippo in the Franklin Park Zoo. He was never late to services. A bottle of rye, scrupulously provided, assured his prompt attendance. An agreement had been made, a glass at the beginning, two at the end.

The drunk's breath grew heavier and shook the dust in a cloud above his nose. A Shalosh Sudoth!

"And Raba said also. . ." It was Chomollofsky, in an ashen whisper. " 'No more than a hair picked out of a bowl of milk.' "

Tsinger roused himself. He sat up in his chair, clicking his thumb against his forefinger. "It reminds me of a joke in Mo'Ed Katon. The Angel of Death met Rabbi Shesheth in the marketplace and requested his soul. 'Please,' said Rabbi Shesheth. 'Not in the marketplace! Let's go home and talk about it.' "

Rappowitz smiled, adding, "Yet Rabbi Nahman asked Raba on his deathbed, 'You know him, nu? Tell him to leave you alone.' What did Raba say?"

"Aaaaaah," gurgled Tsinger, remembering. Rappowitz beat him to it.

" 'Since I lost my muzzel, he doesn't listen to me.' "

Muzzel in the corner awoke. "Nu? Time for trinks?" he asked with a hopeful grin, seeing their smiles.

"Time for some muzzel," quipped Tsinger.

"It's always time for muzzel," the drunk responded gaily.

"We were speaking of Death," said Rappowitz, souring.

"A serious subject," said Muzzel, still smiling, "What did you decide?"

"A hair. . ." They could barely hear Chomollofsky. His frame nodded, a crumbling oak, over the table.

"I remember that passage," Rappowitz said. He brought his hand up to his forehead, sealed his eyes. Swaying, he turned away from Muzzel and began to recite, mumbling out the Aramaic of the commentary in Yiddish. "Raba was at the bed of Rabbi Nahman. He saw Nahman shake, grow rigid, stretching into the arms of Death. 'Tell him to stop!' cried Nahman. 'He squeezes me.'

" 'Aren't you highly regarded?' asked Raba.

" 'Who is regarded, who is esteemed, who is distinguished before the Angel of Death?'

"As Nahman died, Raba whispered, 'Show yourself to me.'

"So in a dream, one night, Nahman came.

" 'Master, did you suffer pain?'

" 'No more than taking a hair from the milk. Yet. . .' "

He paused, his voice heavy, " 'Were the Holy One, blessed be He, to say to me, Go back to the world as you were, I wish it not. . .'

" 'The fear of death is too great.' "

The snap of a twig. Tsinger's fingers. "There's a joke."

The men bent forward to hear, all but Chomollofsky, who was already in that position, his head almost resting on the table.

"The Angel of Death comes to Rabbi Ashi in the marketplace. Out of nowhere he appears and says. . ." Tsinger crooked his finger. Nasty and confidential, the Angel coughed in Tsinger's soprano, "Let's go!"

"Hold on." It was Rabbi Ashi, palm upraised. "I got to arrange my notes. You want a disgrace in Heaven? Let me have thirty days."

"At the end of thirty days comes the Angel.

" 'Let's go!'

" 'What's the hurry?'

" 'Your successor, Rabbi Hunah, is waiting for your place.' "

Tsinger looked around the room. An old joke.

"As for Rabbi Hisda," Rappowitz rocked back and forth, faster and faster. "He could never overcome him. Hisda's mouth was always full, Torah . . . Torah . . . Torah. . . The Angel climbed into a tree, a cedar over the Schoolhouse. The trunk snapped—"

A skull hit the table. No one heard. Rappowitz had clapped his hands.

"Hisda stuttered. His soul was snatched."

"Ah," said Muzzel. "You know of Rabbi Hiyya?" The drunk wet his lips. "Such a man! A real Chochem! When he died, fiery stones fell out of the sky. Gevult! So pious, the Devil could never get near him. What to do, the poor fellow is scratching his brains.

Going meshuggeh. At last, he gets an idea. He dresses up like a Shnorrer, rags, dirty. He comes to Hiyya's house, knocks on the door, asks for a trink."

"Food! He asks for food," Rappowitz interrupted, banging the table.

"For you it's food. I got to have a trink."

"Let him have a drink," said Tsinger.

"He asks for a trink," Muzzel continued. "A glass of schnapps. And they bring it to him. It's a pious household. But the Shnorrer shouts in, 'Nu, Hiyya, you despise the thirsty?' "

"The poor," cried Rappowitz.

"The poor are thirsty," drawled Tsinger.

Muzzel rose in his patched gray overalls. A torn golfing cap was pushed back on his head. His huge brown face tanned in the gutters of Boston shone with the fire of a life of hard liquor. His shadow, dark and swollen, rolled on the wall. Bloodshot, his eyes gleamed.

He shouted, lost in the story, "Hiyya was ashamed! He came to the door himself. He had a glass in his hand and peeked out at the Shnorrer. Nu! At that moment, the Shnorrer pulls out an iron bar, glowing, hot red."

The drunk's fist shook. It burst into flames.

The sun setting behind the broken windows of the ancient chamber burned like a bed of coals and crimsoned the sky, hissing in the sound of a death rattle. Scarlet light filled the room. The old men were struck senseless Dust fell and fell in the silence, collecting on the lids, in the hollowing sockets, of Chomollofsky's eyes.

O breath where have you fled, out of our roofs and tenements, out of our holy books, over the shattered glass, the crumbling wall, our community, the soul of the boatman ascends.

A Sanhedrin of corpses. The Mourners begin the Kaddish, *Magnified and sanctified be His great name. . . .*

GLOSSARY

Shandeh: A shame.
Charpeh: A disgrace.
Shkootz: A corruption of the Hebrew word for Gentile. It carries the connotation of an evil person.
Shkootzim: Many evil Gentiles.
Shalosh Sudoth: The third meal. It takes place between the afternoon and evening service on Saturday—a traditional time to discourse on the weekly portion.
Amalek: "Remember what Amalek did unto thee." Deuteronomy:25:17. The Children of Israel are cautioned never to forget Amalek, a tribe that attacked them in the crossing of Sinai. Saul lost his crown for showing Amalek's king mercy, centuries later. The worst enemies of the Jews are supposed to be descendants of Amalek.
Shvartzas: Blacks.
Goyim: Gentiles, not as pejorative as Shkootzim.
Cushite: Ethiopian.
Shummus: A beadle.
Talmud Chochem: An expert scholar.
Mo'Ed Katon: One of the tractates of the Talmud.
Muzzel: Luck.
Shnorrer: Beggar.
Sanhedrin: A parliament or legislature.

FIVE POEMS

VASKO POPA

Translated from the Serbo-Croatian by Stephen Stepanchev

FAR WITHIN

1

The green gloves rustle
On the branches of the avenue

The evening carries us under our arms
Along a road that leaves no print

Rain falls on its knees
Before gone windows

The yards come out of their gates
And stare after us

2

At the crossroads
The signs of day
Our luck is black and blue

If I turn my head
The sun will fall from its branch

You have buried your smiles
In my palms
How shall I revive them

My shadow grows heavier
Someone is tying its wings

You open your eyes, dear
You hide me without a word
The night looks for me

At the bottom of the avenue
A tree lights a cigarette

3

Without your eyes
There would be no sky
In our blind house

Without your smile
The walls would never fall
From my eyes

Without your nightingales
The willows would never
Cross our threshold

Without your hands
The sun would never
Spend the night in our dream

4

The streets of your regard
Never end

The swallows in your eyes
Never move south

From the aspen in your breast
The leaves never fall

In the sky of your words
The sun never sets

5

Our day is a green apple
Cut in two

I look at you
You do not see me
There is a blind sun between us

On the stairs
Our embrace is broken

You call me
I do not hear you
There is a deaf air between us

Among window displays
My lips search
For your smile

At the crossroads
Our kiss is lost

I gave you my hand
You do not feel it
The void has embraced you

In the public squares
Your tears search
For my eyes

In the evening my dead day
Meets your dead day

Only in dream
Do we walk the same country

DUCK

A waddler in the dust
Where fish do not go
She carries as she lists
The unease of water

Quite unprepared
The waddler is slow
As she moves through dust
Toward an imaginary reed

Oh never
Never will she learn
To walk in dust
As easily
As she once plowed mirrors

SOW

Only when she heard
The mad knife at her throat
Did the red curtain
Define the dance
And she regretted
That she had stirred
From the embrace of the puddle
And had run happily
Happily toward the yellow gate

HORSE

Ordinarily
He has eight legs

Between his jaws
A man had lodged himself
With all the four quarters of his earth
Then he had bloodied his muzzle
He had wanted
To bite through a stalk of corn
That was long ago

In his beautiful eyes
Sorrow has been shut
In a circle
For there is no end to the road
And he must pull
The whole world

THE CHAIR

The fatigue of blundering mountains
Has given an expression
To her sleepy flesh

Forever on her feet

How happily she would
Run down a flight of stairs
Or dance
Under a crown of moonlight
Or simply sit
Sit in someone else's circle of fatigue
To rest

MONTEFIORE

DENNIS SILK

Part I

Moses Montefiore, the meliorist, landed at Jaffa in 1875. He was ninety-one, it was his seventh journey to Palestine. Dr. Loewe his polyglot trotted beside him. He translated the compliments. A lot of people waved poems or petitions. It was wet, his cheque-signing hand held an umbrella. His hat shone on Palestine.

His carriage of good luck shone, also. Montefiore wore English boots and an English hat, he looked an English worthy. But his carriage wheels conjugated in Hebrew, its cushions had never spoken a good Church Latin. It was a black angel-beetle that flew off Montefiore to the blood-libels. Then he would send a telegram to a Palmerston. For Montefiore took off his hat to his past but bowed to Victoria. He was a Victorian worthy, that is he sat like Solomon at board meetings of the Alliance Gas Company.

The quayside shone with good luck. He was the prince of amelioration. He had so many pockets. A pocket glowed with tokens of his dead Judith. Another flared with bank drafts but it was very wet in Jaffa.

Advice

Strange to have such conversations with Judith. Perhaps the Hebrew wheels helped. They travelled through orange groves. His beautiful deceased seemed to know such a lot about everything.

She smiled out through the window at Palestine. "There's such a lot to do, Monte," she said, as though the everlasting veil had been lifted, here among un-English dunams. His wheels had a regular rhythm of their own, but it chimed very well with the serious gossip of Judith. "When you get to Jerusalem, don't forget to see Auerbach and Salant, they'll give you such good advice." Then she went out through the window, he could see her running very fast through the orange grove.

The Tent

The tent walls stared down in gravity on the improvised life of his tent. They covered themselves with portraits of his dead. Almost his entire generation stared down at Montefiore from the other town. Perhaps, in his seven journeys to Palestine, he had been remembering them, serving them as best he could in his shiftless life. He sat there, perhaps studying a balance sheet, before a portrait of Judith. A tall man, he sat there looking at Judith. Every night this staring session, this calling down or going back. The dead woman perfumed his sober wardrobe.

Marking-Ink

Mother marked his underclothes before sending him off to boarding school. M O S E S M O N T E F I O R E. They looked lonely on his bed, the marked-off vests.

Their coach travelled through fields parcelled off from each other. It couldn't join the cut-off townships. "There are deathbeds under the earth where no one visits you."

Stuck

He was stuck between orange groves. He heard some gloomy pump. Its heartbeat clashed with the unbalanced life of his thoughts. Then a moon threw her long and dark shadow from behind a rock. Montefiore's moon of loneliness showed him the way.

Town Plan

He was looking for the town plan. Perhaps a small travelling moon could help him. A moon big as a pony. Perhaps he had bluffed Jerusalem, which held its breath, and hoped. Perhaps he was travelling toward a dead woman in a boat from which he issued statements. Perhaps he wanted a waterwheel to dream by, and he wasn't the prince, any more, of amelioration. A travelling moon over the heads of his horses. Then the waves of travel cover you.

Part 2

Naval Engagement

In this dream, he was standing by the waterwheel in Jaffa. He wore the uniform of a militia captain. Dr. Loewe mocked his pose. No, Loewe, said Montefiore, first of all Napoleon, then the Turk. Guess what I'm thinking under my buttons. The Pasha of Jerusalem is waiting to be watered. We'll sail in by Jaffa Gate.

A Jerusalem Treat

The drawn-up Turks presented arms. They vociferated their huzzas Moorish fashion. He was pleased with their turnout, and said so to the Pasha. The ever-ready exertions of the Turkish Government to make the subjects of the Sultan happy had always pleased him.

They'd prepared a special treat for Montefiore. The Pasha stuck pins into a war-map of the moon. His Turks stared through a telescope at her, shook fists at her, stamped their feet spitefully. Priming their muskets, they aimed them at the moon.

The Bashi-Bazouks' Supper

They shot down the great moon. She was defenceless outside Jaffa Gate. The Bashi-Bazouks scooped up her living pieces. The next thing, thought Montefiore, they'll start on my horses. But the juggling moon laughed at the Bashi-Bazouks. He saw in the sky someone no one was eating. "They're not eating that one," he said in joy to the Pasha. "No, no, not that moon."

More Advice

He'd gone to get good advice from Salant and Auerbach. But they were in a queer mood. "Look." Auerbach pulled back the curtain and pointed at the crescent moon. "She's out again."

Charitable Societies

He was going over their accounts with Auerbach and Salant. They came to the Society for the Promotion of the Return of the Crown to Its Former Position. It seemed to have very few assets. The accounts didn't balance and he queried them with an unusually silent Auerbach.

"There are certain irregularities, certain unusual dispositions of our funds, Sir Moses."

"Not, of course, that you would disapprove of them," added Salant.

"The Rabbis of Jerusalem amaze me at last. Thirty-three years of diligent correspondence, and at last a mystery."

"You are not displeased, Sir Moses?"

"I am delighted. Of course, on condition that you offer me a key to the cipher."

A faint flicker of Auerbach's former disquiet.

"It is easy to see you are tired, Sir Moses. Perhaps, tomorrow, we can go deeper into the transactions of the Society!"

"Certainly tomorrow. Tell me, who is your President?"

Auerbach crossed to the window. "I thought I heard someone listening outside."

"Just a gecko, Rabbi Auerbach, an inquisitive gecko."

The Visit

The next day they called for him with a sedan chair kindly lent by Bishop Gobat—the only sedan chair in Jerusalem. A kavass took them deeper into the city, the petitioners and poem-presenters dropping away. Perhaps because of the heat, or his weight of years, Montefiore had stopped thinking about anything at all. The kavass drew attention, not to an old worthy being carried through khans, but to the earth he pounded.

He had to be carried in the sedan chair up rather a high flight of stairs. A Negro slave came out and helped him in by one arm, Rabbi Salant held the other. He was helped into a room furnished entirely *à l'Orient*, without chairs or tables, straw mattings being laid out in every direction, all nice and clean. The Negro ran into a room leading off, made an enquiry in a low voice, ushered Montefiore into that room. The hangdog rabbis brought up the rear.

The President of the Society for the Promotion of the Return of the Crown to Its Former Position sat in a high-backed chair behind a desk of piled-up correspondence, some of it, Montefiore realised, in his own hand. He saw his massive signature, rising to meet him in Hebrew. The President, wearing nicely tied lace at her neck, gave him her hand.

Dribble

An old man carrying a rain cloud up a staircase, a blackamoor running toward a queen. Sit down, maybe, and say nothing. A table where the rabbis bow.

Sit down, maybe. He took off his top hat, ridiculous in Jerusalem, dug from it a rabbit, danced the jig of a seventeen-year-old boy he had once known, juggled with the lemons on her table, produced a joker from his sleeve, regretted all the letters he had signed in his life, spoke in short sentences. Ninety-one years of dribble. Say nothing.

Weather

Say something.
Hum hum.
Something.
The weather is exceedingly fine.
Something.
Madam, I take off my hat to you.
Something.
Madam, that lace is exceedingly fine.
Something.
Victoria would applaud your lace.
Something.
Your lace and the weather are exceedingly fine.

Viva of the Beloved

Who are you?
I'm ninety-one years stuck on a staircase.
Montefiore, who are you?
My beloved is mine, and I am Montefiore.

Spite of the Beloved

I remember a London apprentice. You're not him. You have an overcoat look, a spinach look, I think you look comfortable, Montefiore.

His hand no longer made the gesture in air of signing cheques. Auerbach and Salant went home, he sat on.

Five O'Clock
Signatures seethed in the five o'clock light of her room. Only Auerbach and Salant to help. The blackamoor brought in jam, and a samovar. Salant and Auerbach. Downstairs the town bought lungs at the butcher.

Important Document
The moon, or a girl, washed her hair. The moon, or a girl, did not wash her hair. The moon and a girl washed their hair.

Fledgling
The queen flew round the room. It was late, it was very late. She was the eight o'clock moon, she was the ten o'clock moon, she was getting later.

PART 3

Naming the Queen
Of course, when he next visited his rabbis, they were as usual watching the moon through a telescope.

"Allow Sir Moses the telescope," said Auerbach. "It is a crescent Matronita, Sir Moses," he added.

"She is a very great lady," Salant said, gently.

Montefiore stared up at his new Judith. She was a pure crescent. "My Matronita," he thought, "not theirs."

"But a little confused from being always alone, a little wild, you might say," said Auerbach.

Montefiore thought of that moon, bent over the ledgers of her Society. Not their moon but his moon.

Lost in partisanship, he hadn't heard what Salant was saying. "I'm sorry, Rabbi Salant!"

"Sometimes, if you listen hard, you can hear her under the town, very deep down probably, under the street, punting under Jerusalem, under all the stone. That's what I had to say."

Sun

The sun was for labour, it got into the syntax of his ten thousand letters: enquiries, replies to replies to enquiries. It came into the room, now, with Loewe. The sun etc. My tragedy for today, he said, and sighed.

Patronage

All the petitioners were amiable and chatty. Someone had come about that garden in Jaffa. Three men wanted to learn weaving in Preston. The town asked to be tried out. He gave his repeater for repairs. The lithographer worked all night on his address cards. The goldsmith's forehead shone all night with intelligence.

Charity

The soup-kitchen ladies tried their soups on him. He ate their giblets sweetly, noodles also, he admired these helpers of the poor. But he himself felt needy. He'd been deprived of distance. Panicking among ladles, he sent the delegations home with great sums.

The Soup Kitchen

This soup kitchen was for thirty poor and old unmarried men. It must be full of nutrition, Montefiore thought. He imagined those thirty shuffling around, removing lids when no one was looking. Not even widowed men, in gaunt Jerusalem, their laces not tied by Matronita.

Baksheesh

An old idol in a sedan chair, he dropped a silver coin in a Turkish hand. For the Turk guarded the door. The sedan chair went up and through. An idol stared at this and that. The Turk laughed behind his hand. Baksheesh in the unwashed hall. Montefiore didn't laugh. Really, the sedan chair carried a weeper. Bishop Gobat didn't know that. The Jew of the m'lords wasn't really theirs. He hadn't been enfranchised by them.

Pickaxe

They took his old bones down to Silwan. Dr. Loewe sat beside him, a chatterbox talking about Amharic in the heat. Montefiore felt he ought to be gratified. This was the habitat for an old meliorist.

Here gecko and Matronita clicked their tongues at each other. The carriage jogged by the half-savage inhabitnats of Silwan. They jostled it for baksheesh. A young bully boy shook the carriage in this silence now broken. The coachman gave him a shove, and they continued under heaven. They passed the tomb of Absalom. It was customary to pelt the tomb of that ambitious son. Montefiore laughed and picked up some stones. "You know, Loewe, it is myself I am stoning. Yes, dear Loewe, I'm stoning ninety-one years of rectitude and fudge. Anyway, it was good to escape the soup kitchen, Loewe."

Loewe helped him to a hillside perch. They could hear peevish runners scouring the area, calling, "Sir Moses, Sir Moses, Sir Montefiore." Their voices were easily disposed of by the valley. He sank into the great Kidron silence, which was broken by the regular rhythm of a pickaxe. Then Judith, closer and insistent. "Coffee and lemonade at the British Consul won't help you, Monte. You're not in that London where teas are given!" The pickaxe continued its attack, its rhythm annoyed him terribly. Then a regular soothing sound of Judith stroking her dog, running her hand along its flanks. She was murmuring, luckily not in the pickaxe rhythm, "Monte's a good boy, Monte's a good boy." It didn't seem strange though he had been wearing long trousers now a good while.

Gihon Spring

The steps were slippery going down to Gihon. But the Silwan people called it Mother of Steps. He listened to her calm breathing. Doubtless it persisted all night. He couldn't hear it while he slept. But if her breath stopped he would die. It recalled for him the steady throb of Nissan Bak's press, donated to him by Montefiore thirty years back. It had been the first Hebrew press in Jerusalem. When it stopped work for the night, an unusual silence filled the printshop floor. But his breath was intermittent. He was a hero of the intermittent. The mother took a calm breath. Into that calm breath miners advanced with their mattock sound, doing the best they could to imitate its regularity. They had followed the breath of the moon into the cutting she made through the mountain. They had mined her valuable white. Hearing her voice, the miners veered in the tunnel, mad to reach her, leaving a line of madness to wonder at.

Mother of Steps
Under the doorstep of the mother, under the Mother of Steps the idea of the town flowed. When the idea of the town failed in her mind, Jerusalem failed, as it did every so often. It became a sadness.

Fire and tears under the step, Jerusalems wavered in the water. The mother retrieved her idea, bent and took her child out of the water. Laid out her negative to dry in the sun.

Part 4

Animal
He was having trouble with his ear. There was an animal scratching away at his eardrum. It seemed very securely in possession, scratching away regularly, keeping its time not Montefiore's. It couldn't tolerate the conversations of a meliorist. It tolerated only sequences of sound. Hum hum said Montefiore. His animal paid not the slightest attention.

His mouth set grimly in lip service. He would have liked to take this animal out of his ear. But maybe it was there before his eardrum, maybe it was his first ear.

Rhythm
The countinghouse rhythm, and the rhythm of his coach-and-four, were the nearest Montefiore had approached to real rhythm. Perhaps, also, at his Gateshead synagogue, in the half-understood Hebrew of his prayer book, he had arrived, via a mumbling of prayers by rote, at a real prayer measure. But all he had known, it now struck him, was the false periods of a guildhall speech, or a Speech from the Throne, or a welcome at the top of some embassy staircase. Cackle cackle for dinner.

The Loom
It was in a workshop that blocked off a courtyard at the side of Bab-al-Salsileh. You walked through pumpkin sellers to get there. Montefiore observed the perfect stillness of a pumpkin. The loom's clack-clack sounded like a dreamy train journey. White strands

jerked back before submitting to the penetration of the weft. The two cotton-rhythms mixed with the journey-rhythm. The cloth (for shrouds, said Loewe) was snipped by scissors into the right shape. Montefiore was mastered by the clack. A clack, a moon.

The Signature

Over the whole town the sound of the pickaxe.

He sat there like an old man at the waxworks. It was difficult for the runners from Hebron, from Nablous, Safat, and Tiberias to realise that the man toward whom they had been hurrying still drew breath. Figures hung from rooftops surrounding the square, speechless before the old meliorist. The poems and petitions had stopped.

Someone from Nablous placed an "important" document on the table. Montefiore looked at him vaguely. "Yes, my dear sir, what do you want of me?" "Your signature, Sir Moses."

He picked up his pen and hesitantly began to write out his name. "Moses," he stopped for a moment but collecting himself continued, "Matronita." Dr. Loewe began to cry.

Plantations

He'd stayed in his hotel two days of rumour for the town. He clicked his tongue at the gecko, liked windows a lot. He hadn't said much to Dr. Loewe. The runners had all gone home. They had eaten their sandwiches. Inside the room he summoned his carriage. A mountain opened its side for him. It was lit by courtesy of the Alliance Gas Company. He stopped now and then to plant a graveyard while his horses flicked tails at flies. They trotted past the Al-Arab Hotel, Nissan Bak's press throbbed through the window. Judith appeared at the window. Beside her several of Nissan Bak's dead workers. Monte, she said, raise your hat to all the kind people. He gladly acknowledged them. Stock Exchange friends didn't seem much. All that hum hum and hum-drum. He had been living in a very frivolous society.

PART 5

Eclipse
She'd gone away. Auerbach and Salant greeted him with the news. They seemed almost pleased at his dismay. Her blackamoor said she'd gone off with a travelling bag, leaving no message.

Chorus
He didn't suppose he would see her again. The staff of the kavass pounding his way helped to indicate the pauses in an elegy. The town composed it. Had she died? No, he was dead for her. The pickaxe sound from Silwan, the tinsmith beating tin for his new trunk, the ouwa ouwa of the Arab porter warning his way, the throbbing of the Nissan Bak Press, pleased and crazed him.

A Fortune
He'd signed away a fortune—syllables, bits of himself, all made out to her. The square had arranged itself around the newly dried ink of this fact.

Town-Sound
A slow lapping under knives and forks, under four regular meals a day. It dissolved the lemonade at the British Consul. Hoist me a sound, he said.

A pestle mixed with the herb it crushed. He was fragrant but could hardly breathe. His intermittent gills found their way through the sea of Jerusalem.

The Noble Enclosure
He was carried to the Noble Enclosure through the Cotton Bazaar. He interrupted his progress to look at the Turkish Bath. It had one attendant, and a phlegmatic Nubian smoking behind a curtain. The drain water frightened him. He got back into Bishop Gobat's sedan chair. A veiled woman watched him climbing up. Adon HaYahud, Adon HaYahud, she called out, mocking, to the old man.

The Enclosure light dazed him after its successive coats of dirt into the Bazaar. Braided sailors, preceded by officers, chattered their way in French through the Dome of the Rock. How gratifying, he thought, and he tried his French on them. Someone introduced himself as Admiral Pâris, he was taking the Mediterranean Squadron around Palestine. Mutual esteem. Gestures of guides accompanied them to the Rock. It seemed a very eminent rock to Montefiore, worthy enough to be discussed in his next communication to his friends at Gateshead. Here Ibrahim would have sacrificed his son but left only his footprints. A Well of Souls was under this rock. There was a lot of water under this rock. Admiral Pâris politely demurred.

Rushy mats were spread round the Rock. For no special reason, umbrella-like plants sprouted from hutches. A grotesque canopy overshadowed the sailors' rushlights. He would have liked to volunteer a sum for a new one. Wisely he decided against. He and his gifted chatterbox stared gloomily at the sealed Rock. It refused to disclose itself. It was rock, not the indispensable element H_2O. The woman-waters were sealed off. Even Judith's nagging and longed-for voice had gone home.

Again

The Rock can't be ploughed with your light plough at Gateshead, Monte. Don't be such a sobersides, Monte. You do look after yourself, you know. Do you want to sit down again with Prince Paskewitch? Asparagus, ices, salad, and dessert.

Rowing

The old man rowed vigorously toward the Temple. It was very hot in the boat. Dr. Loewe took off his frock coat, and sighed. He would have liked, perhaps, to nibble a lettuce. Why were all the landlubbers gawking at Montefiore? It was his sea, now. Scandal to Gateshead Jews. Scandal, even, to Loewe. He wanted to jump out of the boat, to disavow, after so many land-miles, his master. He recalled he couldn't swim.

Montefiore Under

Montefiore: Mosques, and shafts. (Disappearing under.) That's how the world goes.

Loewe: I'm the colour of the abyss. I've translated myself. It's no laughing matter.

Montefiore: Then ask her for help. Call out, Matronita, hold me above your water.

Loewe: Matronita, hold me above your water.

Laying a Foundation Stone

He inspected every one of the houses, went round the boundary of the entire crescent of Mea Shearim, spoke to the children, examined the cistern. They showed him a photographic plan of the estate. Why a cistern? asked Montefiore. He lay on all fours and listened to the pounding earth. Everyone felt a little embarrassed.

Milk of Her

Could he again be a smiling alderman? Temporary light, aldermanic day. He knew why the British Consul was her boy. A procession of staffs pounded the street for her, Reverendissimos of Jerusalem under her window. Whistling and gongs and Ramadhan cannon. Gongs and tongues and river-looms. Milk of her at Gihon.

Dreams

In his first dream, lions destroyed the several floors of a great house. Where there were floors you saw only lions, and the sky coming through. The great rooming house had been cleaned out by lions.

In his next dream, he saw a ship against a receding sea. Representatives of the town were lined up on the shore, a meek crew of millers, bakers, and shoemakers, acknowledging the truth of the sun's setting.

Town-Sound

The dead workers of Nissan Bak printed black-bordered announcements of the town's going. A regiment of kavasses pounded at the town-stone. A cough was a great thing. In this conspiracy against the second ear, Montefiore heard his scratchy quill writing out its last cheque. His signature was torn-up paper in the sky.

The Syrian Print

In this print the steed of Mohammad, Al Barak, with a woman-head and peacock wings, flew from the Kaaba to the Noble Sanctuary. She was the queen of the Sanctuary, patrolled it, had her staging-posts at the Kaaba and the Rock, her wings covering the town and the faithful. She was a little flaccid in the print, a kind of pastry queen with thick lips and marcelled hair. Doubtless in that first print, back in Damascus, in that original Syrian print, she justified her place in the story. The horse with the head of a woman had hooves to kick at the towers she flew by, to maintain a thread of fear from the Kaaba to the Rock. With her thicket of peacock wings she occupied the print.

The Moon in Triumph

He took his ninety-first year down to Gihon. He'd given Loewe the slip. Poor Loewe left alone with his lexicon! Montefiore was anxious to get somewhere. The narrow Gihon cutting hurt his side. He held a candle, at every drip round a bend he imagined an enemy. He was looking for the well-known Matronita animal. The water was up to his waist. The tunnel got lighter but not toward its end. The moon in triumph was whipping his horses at him. They neighed in recognition. She aimed his carriage at him. His wheels chattered angrily in Hebrew. They crushed his hat. Pity an old meliorist with his mouth full of water. You in our wheels, said his carriage. You in my blood, said Montefiore.

FIVE POEMS

AL YOUNG

LONELINESS

The poet is the dreamer.
He dreams that the clock stops
& 100 angles wandering wild
drift into his chamber
where nothing has been settled

Should he get himself photographed
seated next to a mountain
like Chairman Mao
the real sun flashing golden
off his real eyes
like the light off stones
by oceans?

Give me your perfect hand
& touch me simply with a word,
one distillation of forever

Should he put his white tie on
with his black shirt
& pass himself off as a docile gangster
for the very last time?

The poet's dream is real
down to the last silver bullet

Should he slip again to Funland
in the city & throw dimes down holes
to watch hungry women flicker
one hair at a time
in kodacolor
from sad civilized boxes?

Should he practice magic
on politicians &
cause them to crack their necks
in a laughing fit?

The poet is the dreamer.
He dreams babies asleep in wombs
& counts the wasted sighs
lost in a flake of dusty semen
on a living thigh

Should he dream the end of an order,
the abolition of the slave trade,
the restoration to life
of dead millions
filing daily past time clocks
dutifully gorging themselves
on self-hatred & emptiness?

Should he even dream
an end to loneliness,
the illusion that
we can do without

& have no need
of one another?

It is true that he needs you,
I need you,
I need your pain & magic,
I need you now more than ever
in every form & attitude–
gesturing with a rifle in your hand
starving in some earthly sector
or poised in heavenly meditation
listening to the wind
with the third ear
or staring into forever
with the ever-watchful third eye,
you are needed

The poet is the dreamer &
the poet is himself the dream
& in this dream
he shares your presence

Should he smash down walls
& expose the ignorance
beneath our lying noisiness?

No! No!
the gunshot he fires
up into the silent air
is to awaken

BIRTHDAY POEM

First light of day in Mississippi
son of laborer & of house wife
it says son on the official photostat

not son of fisherman & child fugitive
from cottonfields & potato patches
from sugarcane chickens & well-water
from kerosene lamps & watermelons
mules named jack or jenny & wagonwheels,

years of meaningless farm work
work Work WORK WORK WORK–
"Papa pull you outta school bout March
to stay on the place & work the crop"
–her own earliest knowledge
of human hopelessness & waste

She carried me around nine months
inside her fifteen year old self
before here I sit numbering it all

How I got from then to now
is the mystery that could fill a whole library
much less an arbitrary stanza

But of course you already know about that
from your own random suffering
& sudden inexplicable bliss

THE PROBLEM OF IDENTITY

Used to identify with my stepfather first making me want to be a gas station attendant simple drink coca-cola listen to the radio, work on people's cars, hold long conversations in the night black that clean gas smell of oil & no-gas, machine coolness, rubber, calendars, metal sky, concrete, the bearing of tools, the wind–true Blue labor Red & White

Identified with Joe Louis: Brown Bomber, you know Theyd pass along the mud streets of Laurel Mississippi in loud speaker truck, the white folks, down by where the colored schools was and all of us, out there for Recess or afterschool are beckoned to come get your free picture of Joe Louis, *C'mon & get it kids it's Free, c'mon naow*–What it is is chesterfield cigarettes in one corner of the beautiful slick photo of Mr Louis is the blurb, *Joe Louis like to smoke too, see, and he want all yall to follow right long in his footsteps & buy up these here chesterfields & smoke your little boodies off & youll be able to step up in that ring begloved & punch a sucker out* It was the glossiness of the photo, I finally figured out years later, that had me going–didn't really matter whose picture was on it altho it was nice to've been Joe's because he was about as great as you could get downsouth, post world war II as the books say

Identified with Otis (think his name was) worked at grocery store in Ocean Springs, came by, would sit & draw on pieces of brown paperbag, drew in 1940s style of cartoons bordering on "serious" sketching, i.e. in the manner of those sultan cartoons with the harem gals you see em all the time in old Esquires & Playboys Well, that's the way Otis could draw & he'd show me in the make-do livingroom seated on do-fold how to do a portrait of a chic perfect anglo-featured woman, say, in profile out of his head built mostly from magazine & picture-show impressions, & he could draw lots of world things, drew me for instance

Later Otis went up to Chicago, sadness, madness, wed, bled, dope, hopeless, catapulted into the 20th century like the rest of us–rudely,

steeped in homemade makeshift chemical bliss of/or flesh, waiting for nothing less than The Real Thing

DEAR OLD STOCKHOLM

Of course it is snowing
but two city girls,
one blonde the other black-

haired, are preparing for bed
in a warm apartment they share.
One is washing her hair in the bathroom sink
while the other does her hatha yoga exercises.
They have been dancing with some young men
who spoke nothing but north american english,
one of them from Pittsburgh
(from crawfords grill up on the hill)
& the other
a fingerpopper from Leamington, Ontario.

Suddenly, recalling the evening,
the rushing from taxis up inside music clubs,
all of them pleased that it should be so,
the bathroom blonde
who,
like a great many scandinavians,
played some instrument in secondary school
whistles John Coltrane's whole solo
from the Miles Davis *Dear Old Stockholm*
which had been an old swedish folk song.
In fluorescent abandon
& in time
she massages her foamy scalp
with delight.

The young black-haired woman
hearing all this
—tensed in a shoulderstand,
head full of blood,
filling with new breath—
is overcome with unexpected happiness.

Each girl smiles in private
at the joyfulness of the evening
& at the music & the men, wishing
it would never end

MAYA

The life I've led
keeps me from committing suicide
—BLAISE CENDRARS

Songbirds gigging all across California
zipping past slowed-down lenses of the waking eye
dont know this bird
a bird more me than shadows I cast
the moon tonight
as fat as a goose
flashing all thru me
funnybird that zooms
like a feeling
straight up
to escape the heart's net
winging
        winging
                further yet
even beyond tantrums
the world throws
aimed at crippling creatures in flight

Sweet tourists of the soul
there never flew a cockatoo
there never was a tiger cub
there never was an antelope
never a vanishing spermwhale
that leaped or dove
more longingly than I
for love
up into that clean white sky
of the eye's mind

There never lived an Asian brother
or Bantu lover
or Cherokee
whose love of floating surpassed my own

Merciful Kali
Bringer & Taker-Away of feathers & bricks
bring me to the true & lasting route to joyfulness
that I may forsake the use of filthy drugs
& not misuse this gift of speech

THE STORY OF A STORY

PAUL FRIEDMAN

When the conclusion of a certain kind of story is so powerful that it will blot out all else, to tone that down, to keep the conclusion from overshadowing the full body of the story, any one of several possible devices may be employed. A successful technique the writer of serious fiction sometimes uses when faced with this is foreshadowing. In Faulkner's "A Rose For Emily," Emily holds onto her lover's body for years; this is discovered at the end. To in part counteract the sensational aspect of that revelation, we learn early in the story that, out of anguish and grief, she, on the death of her father, refused for several days to give his body up for burial. Somehow that helped prepare the reader for the shock at the end. When faced not only with a powerful ending but with a plot so engrossing it will call undue attention to itself if not somehow tempered, the author may simply begin with plot summary. In Hawthorne's "Wakefield," where a man walks out of his house and away from his wife for twenty years, lives in the house around the corner, and then, for no apparent reason, returns, we get all this in a single paragraph. After that Hawthorne goes ahead and replays that one paragraph, now taking many pages to fill in the story.

With my story it's not necessarily the impact of the conclusion or the magnetic quality of the plot but, if you will, the patness of it all that makes me wary. It may seem overly contrived, too blatantly manipulated, all the strings are tied together at the end: it may not be fictionally believable. I'm ruler, king, creator, god, in short, Paul Friedman, author. I could change the end and that would eliminate the need to go into all this, but I reject that. There are a variety of reasons for my doing so, some of which will shortly out; for now let's simply say I choose to experiment.

No changing. No summarizing (summary blunts interest in the plot). No foreshadowing (foreshadowing dulls the impact of the conclusion). Authors, when they give up, for instance, impact, hope to gain more than they give. I've warned that this ties up neatly; that costs me something. By reminding you that this is fiction, not fact, I'm giving up the illusion of reality; authors work to achieve just that. A widely held tenet in the world of reality is that once something exists or happens, it, therefore, automatically exists or has happened. Mere occurrence is proof conclusive; degree of improbability, matters of implausibility immediately become immaterial. The inconceivable unquestionable is, if it turns out to be. It's only in the fictional world—the world I live in—that the illusion of reality must be achieved. Clearly this totally unrealistic criterion we've developed for fiction places an intolerable burden on certain kinds of stories.

I'm giving up the reality of illusion. That costs. That's expensive.

Inevitability. (Pat ending.)

There is the fine kind where the reader after finishing the story says yes, of course, that's the only way it could have ended. Somehow, after the fact, there's the realization of the fact's inevitability.

There is, of course, another kind, finer I think. Terrifying: because you know what is going to happen, you see it coming, you sense it can't be stopped, it can't be prevented even though tragedy will occur. You sit on the sidelines watching, waiting, knowing, helpless.

The King killing.

The shock of King's death. Shocked? Why? Surprised? Why? Didn't we know it was likely he'd be killed? We knew. And the shock came from that: that we knew, and, knowing, still we couldn't stop it, still we didn't prevent it.

How feeble, how weak, how puny. The shock deals with that, our own fallibility, our own mortality: Each time we face that truth it's a fresh jolt:

Pat.

I'm author. In control. I guide. Geometric correctness. King's death had that: inevitability. Form is one thing but for an author to be a character he has to be content. That's part of the experiment. I'm wary of fictional geometric correctness: What's factually permissible may be fictionally fraudulent: too neat.

Nevertheless, can't you see the fallacy of changing this end; I want to try this; what an opportunity, I'm the author, Paul Friedman, I've never been contented and I'm trying. Inevitably.

I'm a thinker, not a doer.

Exploring interests me, I'm an explorer.

Natural phenomena interest me.

My height interests me. So do my eyes. What do I see? How high am I, I'm curious. I've been asking for years and the only answer I ever get is, Five feet so and so. Crap. Rulers are notoriously inexact.

Measuring sticks are machine made, mass produced, yet you always get an answer to the inch.

If I'm king, nevertheless I grant my kingdom's insubstantial, don't think I have a big head.

What else? My age? You see my predilections, my inclinations.

My thoughts generally aren't startling. How could they be, why should they be? If you're a doer you do, if you're a thinker you think, period. You can cope with the idea of a mediocre mechanic, a dumb doer, why be surprised by a thoughtless thinker? We're surrounded.

I'm a thinker of a kind, a writer: I operate on approximately the level of daydream.

If one were to write about a doer, plot would revolve around doings: joining the Army, fighting a battle, going to town, getting drunk. . . . Writing about a thinker, the plot's made of his mind: with its ins outs ups downs curves edges ledges. A thinker: we pick him up approaching new territory. There's some tension: will he try it, will he plunge in or won't he? If so, will he follow in hot pursuit regardless of where it leads, or will he grant sanctuary beyond some certain parallel of discretion or river of interest?

In. Having plunged, one wonders: will he crack, snap, flip, come out starved, vacant eyed, mute? Or will he emerge smiling, the conqueror, his photo taken as he stands triumphantly with one foot upon the dead carcass of some lionized concept, looking English, will he have his foot on an elephantine notion—in short, some bull?

Many layered: all within.

Mind. Body. (1) Mind. (2) Body. Sometimes in harmony, sometimes warring.

Rendered impotent. Impotence. There's no denying it, the eyes of truth stare you in the face.

The mind, the mind:

To the desk, nine in the morning: start thinking. Stop. Get up, go out, buy a paper. Takes an hour. Ten, coffee. Ten thirty, a letter. Eleven, tempted to lie down for some minutes, only a few, sleepiness, fatigue, eyes heavy, a whole day ahead, mind's blurred, not sharp, can't think. Twelve. Hungry. Eat. One: the news, threat of war, buy a paper and pretend you're seeing what the columnists say. So on through the day. Late at night fatigue gone, sleepiness of the day gone, now last chance, it's a new day, I haven't worked, last chance to sleep: if I want to, it's that simple, if I want to avoid tossing turning twisting, if I want to sleep I have to work. Alert. Door locked. Could, could trick self. Could postpone the trip in, that exploration.

How? Exercise. Do exercises. Mind and body, warring. Partners. Lift weights. Tire body, wear off tension, release energy. Exhaust body. Then sleep. It works, I know. I know. Or, better, work: a while. One idea, one sentence, then, euphoric, jump up grab barbells dumbbells lift pull strain pant sweat grunt more weight pull stretch sleep.

It works.

It works.

It works.

Multi level divisive warfare. Many layered. Us.

This whole notion of intercourse that's been going around for the last decade has done more than anything I know to ruin the pleasures of masturbation.

Or cards.

Here you don't tire the body but dull the mind. Solitaire. Game after game, over and over, endlessly. Eight games, ten games, twenty. Shuffling's a problem. Overcome it, outsmart it, use your head: don't shuffle, collect cards and deal out poker hands, that gets them mixed.

Tricks.

A guess: Sartre would knock forty points off the top of his IQ for four inches of additional height. That's not original, Mailer probably first made the observation. Sartre should have lifted. It's an immense cellular truth: stature counts, stature matters; heights, like realities, exist.

For years I mailed my stories out, they went about, I worried constantly they'd be returned rejected. They were. Mental health's important. One keeps one's body sound, the mind's entitled to the same treatment. I began sending out five originals of the same story: Multiple submission is forbidden. It did wonders, tricks and games. I had to hope my story would not be accepted at two magazines at the same time, I worried constantly it would be. My hopes were constantly fulfilled, my worries never justified.

Writer. Mental health. Mind. Preserved.

Originally I was going to call this, "The Autobiography of My Wife." Then I came up with the current title:

"The Story of a Story"

It's January 2, at the airport.

"Will you love me when I'm back in New York?"

"I'll love you even when you're dead, Grandpa," Karen said.

There was a startled silence.

Now he is dead.

Karen cried, sensing from the silence that she'd said something wrong.

He raised me, but he was not my father.

On the third floor of a high school in the classroom. The door is locked, two boys are holding a third boy by the ankles out the window. He is dangling head first. The bell has not yet rung. The teacher is now trying to get into the classroom but the door is locked and no one's opening up. There's a crowd of students below; they're waiting.

Later, after the boy had been hauled in, after the teacher had been let in, after the class, the boy was asked how he felt toward

Lenny now. Lenny had been one of the two holding him by the ankles. It had been Lenny's idea.

"You must hate Lenny."

"Man, you kidding, you crazy? When he pulled me in the only thing I felt for him was love for not dropping me."

The teacher, who taught little, learned much and left thinking he knew nothing.

My neighbors: women who used to give Tupperware parties, men who bowl on Tuesday and Thursday nights in league. . . . Not quite, but there's truth in that description. Times change. My neighbors invited a John Bircher, just to hear what he had to say, to hear both sides. I talked with him afterward. He frightened me; I lift weights for strength, he talks to God. Martin Lucifer King, communist devil, that sort of thing.

The old chestnut: Eisenhower is for integration, but gradually; Stevenson is for integration, but moderately. It should be possible to compromise between those two extremes: My neighbors.

Once two magazines took the same story. I let it go, I changed the title. I list both when I send out lists. So far so good, no one's noticed.

Whatever made you ask that?
Just something I was thinking about.
You were thinking about that?
Yes.
How come?
I don't know, it just came into my mind.
Come on, get off it, do you expect me to believe that?
Why shouldn't you, it's the truth.
In a pig's eye.
What do you mean?
You wouldn't know the truth if it hit you in the face.
I can't believe this, what's this all about anyway?
Figure it out yourself.

You're a spy, that's what you are, it's the only thing to call you. She was starting in again. Sh, he snapped. Then he said, I remember the first time I went to the toilet with my mouth full of food. I wondered what would happen, I was a kid, six or seven, I wondered what would happen with things going in and coming out at the same time. Give me a piece of paper, I better write that down. That filth, you want to write that down? Yes. You really wondered that, what sort of filthy mind do you have anyway? Actually it just popped into my head but maybe I'll be able to use it sometime. How disgusting. You're such a calculating person, but I wish you'd had the good manners to do that, to make things up instead of spying and putting down exactly what happened.

Stop bullshitting, the only thing you ever made love to was your fist.

Christmas decorations are out, the season of good cheer. I passed a little boy coming home, snot nosed, maybe seven. Teeth chattering, lips chapped. Skinny. Wearing Levi's and wet shoes; a thin jacket. The soft pink flesh of the inner part of his lower lip was divided from the flaking chapped outer part by a thin line of grime. He was throwing snowballs and his fingers were wet and red. He didn't know how cold he was, how blue. A bus was coming, he watched it come, waited, threw two snowballs, hit it twice. Yippee! he yelled. His last snowball, before I turned off, hit the bull's-eye: the middle of a red STOP sign on the corner. He noticed me. Hey mister did you see that? I nodded yes. I'm going to be a pitcher, he said.

He had no idea how frozen he was, or even that he was.

My neighbors, they too are suffering.

I'm a writer, they think I'm interesting.

I finally got that bastard where I want him, by the balls, and now I'm going to squeeze.

Two hills of earth stood a few feet from the shanty—a trailer on blocks. Jerry held the hose low so the old man could pass. The old man stopped, there was something in his hand.

Mr. Steel was the renting agent. Ray Loundes was the super on this ten million dollar job, a seven story luxury apartment house. Tons of dirt had been hauled over by Pacelli Landscaping.

Laborers thinned it by removing weeds with rakes and pitchforks. Then the soil was shoveled into wheelbarrows and pushed to where the shrubbery would be.

Jerry, washing the sidewalk down with the hose, looked at the old man.

They'd been doing it day in and day out for weeks; it was amazing. She was going away for the weekend.

What am I going to do, he said. There was a suggestive leer on his face.

What do you mean?

You know what I mean.

Satisfy yourself.

Sure, great idea, how?

She picked up her luggage.

Jerk off.

Did you let one?

What?

Did you let one?

They'd finished making love.

You always do that.

I have a sour stomach, what do you want from me?

God what a rotten smell.

I get fierce pains if I hold it in, you know that, what do you want from me?

Silence.

Did you let it on me?

No answer.

You did. You let it before you turned around, you weren't turned the other way. What's happening to us? Oh Jesus, what's happened to us?

He gets there late and stands in the huge crowd of jeerers. He sees a sign a high school boy next to him is holding. He sees a big red STOP sign drawn at the top of the boy's sign. He sees only STOP THE WAR, but below WAR it says DEMONSTRATORS. He doesn't see that bottom word. Cursing, he grabs for the sign, saying, What do you mean stop the war? He gets the sign, rips it in half, and throws it to the ground. The boy is stunned. (My sign, my sign.) Legionnaires yell, What are you doing he's on our side. He hears, but he seems unable to comprehend. Then he picks up the two pieces of the sign and holds them together. He says, Oh shit, oh shit I didn't know. He says to the boy, I'm for the war, I'm for the war too, I'm sorry, I'm for the war.

Then someone raises a sign saying, King For President.

"Say, what's it cost a man to have a job like this done?" the old man asked Jerry.

"Oh," Jerry said, then the cement mixer started up and he didn't have to answer.

The old man waited. "How much, about a thousand dollars?"

Jerry washed down the sidewalk. Seeing the old man approach, he'd played the stream of water up the driveway he and his partner had just finished cementing. It had been difficult getting the pitch just right. That was particularly important in the backyard; if the pitch was right the water would roll to the drain and there would be no puddles after a rain. Puddles eroded cement. If water collected ice formed.

"We give out estimates for each job individually, no two jobs are alike. You got a job you want me to take a look at, or you just wonder about prices?"

"Oh, I don't wonder about prices at all. I'd give you a job, I need a new porch put in, I'd give you the job if I thought I'd live long enough to see it done." He waved his hand and there was an envelope in it. "I write my son once a week. You think he cares? I can't get excited." He pointed. "Bum ticker. The doctor told me not to get excited." He looked at the envelope. "I ought to go mail this." He lit another cigarette. "You think he cares if he hears from me or not?"

"Don't you think you ought to take it easy?" Jerry said. "You're getting yourself pretty excited."

"Upset?" He laughed. "You show more interest in me than he does. Christmas is the only time I get to see him and that's if I fly out there." Suddenly he tore the letter up. "How can you help getting excited? Some gratitude." He stared at Jerry, then threw the bits of paper on the sidewalk and walked away.

Tied up. Neatly.

I make myself available. I leave openings.

Contact. Contact is made. Good.

Advice is asked. Given. By the same person. Frequently myself. There are many layers.

I collect. I connect. What? That which counts. That which, in my opinion, counts. I discard, discount, disconnect. I judge. I interpret and clarify. I annotate. I am working on an annotated edition of—you name it.

Exploring interests me, I'm an explorer.

Natural phenomena interest me.

My height interests me. So do my eyes. How high am I? I'm curious. What is there left to tell you, my age?

Grow up.

I'm a thinker in the broad sense, I choose and gather. I collate. I'm a collater. I put together and form new patterns out of old shapes. It's my own peculiar sense of proportion, that's all I have to offer. I sign my own name.

I've just reread these pages. Words and words, lines of lines. I've just reread this fiction. There's an inconsistency of characterization, the characterization's uneven.

Enough. There are elements for a story here. If I were really Paul Friedman I'd write it.

CIRCE

STUART MONTGOMERY

At last we sighted the island
home of the goddess Circe
whose clear voice
dissolves the eyes and ears
of lost sailors and blinds
their hearts with her body

Absolute silence like a ruler
leant over the prow of our black ship
and pulled her into the harbour
where we leapt out on the blinding white
beaches whiter than we knew which drew
our bodies down tired already by the blue sea
we shouted but all sounds died on our lips
and in our ears the singing of thousands
of confused cicadas in the trees was drowned
by the appalling white silence
which threw us onto the sand
to sleep for two nights and two days

On the third morning blue with cold
I crept out as the first red fingers
stretched the dawn in the sky
to explore the lie of the land
belting my sword tight I felt
my spear shaft alert in my hand

From the top of a wide view I saw
the small curl of blue smoke rising
like a warning from a thickset forest
of oak enclosing a house of smooth stone
my frown tightened as I returned to send
Eurilochus with a few of our men

Clumsy feet and cracking sticks
led them to Circe's house of cut
and dressed stone this warm home
of the goddess was set in a clear
zone in the dense folder of trees

Gods leap backwards look
wolves with lolling tongues
ignored our bristling spears
gambolled up to our feet tails
wagging reared up on their
hindlegs and licked our shields
lions rolled on the ground
welcomed these new friends
to their circus of bewitched men

while our men waited, still
as the air
                they could feel
her clear Circe voice emerge like
a moist silver weave needle tracing
song patterns lingering birds in their
swoopings leave for her fingers

to glisten in sprinkling azure
emerald & ebony in
to enter her delicate never ending
fabric of gold & gossamer laughing

Polites pulled by her voice of moist
silver called them to follow him
through her shining doors opened
slowly to beckon them lips
thick with sound into the enchanting

offered them cushions & chairs covered
with skins of soft strange animals then fed
them a mixture of cheese barley black wine
& honey ground to a paste with an extract of
pungent insects so potent & sad it corroded
the spring of their strong tongues sinking
slowly & seeping into their bones to soften
their sharp heartache for their homes

as she clouted them one by one
with her black stick
  bellies swelled
  neck skins bristled
  sniffed their thick
  pigstench saw their
  own & their friends
  hands clench in horror
  and tighten into pigsfeet
clattering across marble floors
she penned them to snout acorns
berries hogsfilthy wallow together

held back by his fears, his distrust of
strange music that loosened his thighs
Eurilochus

cautious of the least pleasure in his five
senses (in particular touch) saw his men
enter the house while he waited outside
with the hours trampling his heart
then slowly returned through
the forest to fetch Odysseus

Belted my armour on, the weight of my
bronze sword cooling my skin. Come
Eurilochus, I said let us ask or
even force her to release them

No, he cried, do not go
her voice is, he said, looser
than music to grapple with
like glue it will swallow you

left him then with the rest
of our men to guard our black ship
and pressed on through the forest
with my heart pounding alone
to the time of my feet to find
the house of dressed stone

a fish eagle circling
the deep blue
                    slow sea
suddenly plunged towards
me saw me and gracefully
switched into a swallow

Hermes
god of omens, broke
open the air, appeared
as a youth with fair
hair & blue eyes, spoke
to me . . . Odysseus

Beware of the curse of her mouth
pursed like a dark song
will hog you to wallow forever
unless you obey my advice

First she will kiss your feet and caress
your tied limbs as you enter her house
seat you and feed a mixture of dangerous
musk past your teeth like a delirious
ghost in your throat she will rise to seize
and anaesthetise your heart

Quick whip your sword out but
touch her only with metal until
        her body
softer than music asks you to
                play with her
but first make her swear not
to sink her lonely teeth permanently into
or in any other way maim you . . . Odysseus

To protect me Hermes reached with ease
through the earth to uproot the black tuber
of molu, the milk white flower
which I chewed
bitter heat overpowered my face
bent close to the smell of the ground
as the God disappeared

Heavy the weight in my chest
heavy my limbs my feet bowed down they carry my arms
my genitals tight can feel
her file her nails the bite
of her teeth will meet the iron
that coats my mouth will taste
will drain the rust in my blood
will darken the rasp on her tongue
will feel the weight in my chest
will strain to beat to beat to beat

With a low voice Circe
with a low voice I called to the Goddess
outside the house I see
her open her doors I see
the marble floors dreading her eyes
dreading her face I see
she led me in I follow her feet
to sit me down on a silver throne
I hold the arms embossed and carved
she kissed my feet caressed my limbs
she mixed her musk in a cup of gold
Drink it down I held the throne
Drink she said in a low command
Drink it down I drink I drink
I drowned my heart I felt it groan
against the tide I felt my feet
my feet are mine secure at last

she strikes at my heart
which beats faster and faster as I
suddenly draw my bare sword hard
against her left breast forced her
to fall at my knees & raise up from the floor
the black opals of her eyes & cry to me

How can a plain seaman like you
resist this darkness I kissed
past your teeth to hurt and
trap your heart squeezed
tap tap in my palm

must be wily Odysseus come
back from Troy to rip up
the savage satin of the sea
Hermes warned me
patiently

to persuade you to ease your sword
in its sheath and let you slide into
me slowly and unwind beside me as
gradually as the sad sea in a storm
breaks quartz into soft layers of sand

Swear first on your sacred curse Circe
not to fasten your tongue or thirsty teeth
into my scrotum drawn in grimly as
the seething sea as I sink into you

Come sailor she said as she pulled my hand
could feel the warm dome of her belly
is firmly moving the sea you are
waves in the sand
outspread wings
in the wind my skin
will swell and fill
in the well in my belly
there
gently Odysseus

where she cried out

this cast iron fist in my chest
is beating my breath
look, I open my mouth
with her mouth and I lie
                with my
tongue by the side of her tongue
which rears
                blue belly swollen
                and subsides
                folded

She lies quiet in her throat song

She lies sleeping round the soft soft body
snug chuckle in her throat fucked a woman laugh
and her smell of her nose softly sway poked in her belly
the full of her eyesmile (Homer said all this happened
in the Spring) the skin warm and smoothing under my hand
buried a hug reappeared no distance which is my side
of the touching

in my hand
a seashell
summons the sea
come down to the beach
with me said Circe

in her
      hands
my body
      became
urgent
      as a
whirlpool
      for her
and
      wrestled
indelibly
      with her
unbelievably
      white
limbs
      under
the sea

caught in the water
                        together

working her mouth
over me
like the sea Circe
and drew
me into her body
together
we breathe the sea
and
swim further
the poem
is a journey
the sea the
surface
by which we re-enter the earth

the one wrestles with the nine
on a desolate beach
how many times did we come
into the arms of the sea
Circe
where have we been together
under the surface of the sea
where have my friends gone
what have you done to them

language has worn
white as wood
scoured bare by the sea
or as white as her hair is
he thought
of the lucid
surface of words
when softer
than
language
she touches it
or hard as his ear when

the sounds she sings ring in
them under the sea then
casts them up as she
casts up men when
she has finished with them

left me
alone
by the shore

a mere
sailor
whose single

blue tears
each
in mingling

like a dream
into
the sea

seemed
to be
dissolving him

the tears of the sailor moisten the sea

the rain
mingling in
her
hair
made him
hear
clearly

the mermaid
in her
murmuring
to him

and again
the murmur
of the sea
he heard
in her
ear
made him
sure
she had
shared
in his sadness

which is
as always
hers
in her
murmuring
and his
also in
his tears
mingling
him
into her

the sea surge
in her seething
urged
his sadness
to the surface
within him
in the shape
of tears

in bursting
into her
thin
blue skin
burnt her
grief into him

the endless murmur
of seabreezes assuming
the voices of trees
sea silk speaking softly
to him like whispering
sea satin in blue cedars
(mermaids they said
are always sad
and their sadness
seeps gradually
into the sea)

certain
sea words
of hers
seemed to be
luring him nearer
the firm curve of her ear
where he heard faintly
her sensuous sea phrases
sway and surge in her slurred
sea speech searching
ceaselessly uneasily
like fish
sea words slip
when
he reached for them

as his arm
reached into the sea
for the root of her tongue
a strong swarm
of little fish brushed
lightly against his lips

the wave
carves through the air
a clear echo
of her
in the curve
blue rows of ears
rise towards the shore
to hear her crumble
and thunder as
another wave raises
gestures and praises

the unguarded
shore
is a graveyard
of waves

black
  boat
rocks
  hopelessly
on the lapping
  blue sea
sky above
  and on the water
shadows
  waver
the dark sky
  moves at night

like water
        over his eyes
focusing them
        on one star
blue as Penelope
        and familiar
as heartbeats
        which filled
his thoughts
        with her
from sleeping
        until waking
making him
        feel so close to her
he slept well

each wave wavers
                as the sea moves
relentlessly
                towards the shore
a few more blows
                measure the four
seasons—the rains came
and violent storms—we say
we will not remain the same
but the rocks and the waves break
the only chung
                or fulcrum
is the island and the pounding
rhythm the words and the waves make
                and their timing
as time and again the shapes
resemble the shape of an old poem
                the writing itself
is part of the process of ageing

THE QUEEN OF SLEEP

CAROL EMSHWILLER

This, the diary of lost sleep. New but not elegant. 3 x 5½. Green plastic cover. 365 pages. I ignore the months. Mark it into eight sections of forty-five days each, each section representing one hour of a normal night's eight-hour sleep. First section: August 31 to October 15. Second section: October 16 to December 1, et cetera. Five days left over at the end of the year.

Each day begins at 11 P.M. with sleep. Any sleep slept before eleven must be counted in the day before. I avoid fractions of an hour. Awkward to add up and unaesthetic if left over at the end of a forty-five-day section. Sleep must be timed carefully even if it means waking up earlier.

Every morning can be a renaissance, but why start with waking? Sleep can be a renaissance too. Each of my days begins, then, with sleep and if only I could anticipate the exact instant when I drop off, or if I could count backward from five to one and be asleep, how much easier all this would be.

Signs to use in this book: o for sex, x for menstrual, √ for a happy day, and √√ for when three hours or more ahead on sleep.

Money: Pay myself a dollar for every hour of sleep over eight. Spend the money on those five last days of the year. Eat favorite foods. Go to favorite spots. See a movie. Dance.

But money isn't lost for sleeping less than eight hours because I will have lost enough already with the lost sleep. (And if I should stay good tempered in spite of it all?)

Keep track of disposition. Take an APC pill. Exercise ½ hour a day. Take a hot bath.

These sleep dollars will be more completely mine than any others I earn. One could say they are twice-earned dollars. They can be wasted. They can be squandered on two copies of the same thing: two *Marshlands* by Gide, two blue necklaces, or two presents for the same person, even three. That's why I'm celebrating August 31. New Year's Day for me. My little green book. But I wonder if the weather can be the cause of this sense of euphoria, or the moon, or perhaps the pituitary gland instead of the start of my year. (Do I dare to throw away my old notebook yet?)

Days are growing shorter. Nights are growing longer all over the top half of the world. By December even the Arabs wake up in the dark.

Waking on a bright November morning, I needed you. I have stayed up all night for you. I have waited, tense on my bed while you didn't come. I have slept yesterday's sleep tomorrow and waked with a smile in spite of it and counted up my hours. I haven't paid myself a dollar for a week. New resolutions are useless. I write this letter:

> Dear E.
>
> I loved you again. I was in love with you all day. I felt it coming on yesterday. I was all warmth and dependence. Oh, why aren't you ever here at the right times! I could have been so nice. I could have been everything you've always wanted, anything you've wished for, but by the time you came back it was over. If only I hadn't waked up so early this morning, it all might have happened later.
>
> Best wishes. (Dare I write, love?)

Love fades hour by hour. I think he has sucked at my earlobe once too often.

I think that the sick lie down, the dead lie down. People with headaches or sore feet. People making love usually lie down.

From the tightrope of sleep one can fall suddenly into wakefulness at any moment. From the table of sleep one can reach and touch the floors of reality with one finger or toe, because sleep, compared with death, is waking.

Love increases hour by hour and what I need now is somebody to tell things to. I've met the first chair flute player of the symphony orchestra. I will tie my blouse up in front so my belly button shows, but what's his opinion of green capes and short hair? Those dresses with holes along the sides may help, but he can't practice while I'm eating and he'll have to keep quiet when I think about what my future courses of action should be. And, thinking of that, I've written down the address of where you write to donate your eyes after you die (one of my possible contributions to society) but I'd rather do something entirely different. Give them a piece of my brain, the part that thinks about life-in-general, the core of myself as *femme moyenne sensuelle* if there is such a thing as a sensitive every-woman. Sometimes I doubt it, because if there is, who is she? Someone certainly untroubled by menstrual fluctuations (I allow myself an afternoon nap on my bad days of the month and this, added to the sleep hours, should put me ahead with my dollars).

Do they stare at me in my dress with the holes along the sides? I don't stop to wonder. It's the sort of thing I can think over later when I'm alone on the evenings when I wonder if my stomach sticks out. I can't hold it in more than a few minutes at a time but I've tried to whenever I was side-view to anyone important. Do I eat too much?

The flute player might answer all my questions. I know I could do what *he* wants me to (if he would only tell me what he likes). I write:

> Dear F. P.
>
> I could love you if you looked at me while you were playing in the orchestra and I was sitting in the second row and this was Vivaldi night. I hope you will tell me what you want me to do. I'm prepared for anything.
>
> Best wishes. (Dare I write, love?)

New signs to use in this book: & for a night spent listening for footsteps. * for sleeping all my sleep before 1 P.M. ∞ for infinity, as in infinite loveliness. Flute players have quick hands.

Things I like about flute players: Flute player noses, flute player lips. The strength of their little fingers. Breath on my neck. Sharp elbows. Black silk socks. I find flute players blowing into holes in beer cans and into the tops of coke bottles or with pieces of grass between their thumbs. What I like about flute players is how they can say *u* umlaut.

I'm keeping all my resolutions after all. I'm coming out ahead on sleep. With my first twice-earned five dollars I will buy the flute player a present. It's for his sake I overslept this morning.

This euphoria has finally been identified as resulting from two cups of coffee in quick succession on an empty stomach. I suppose it's best just to ignore it. It may not last much longer anyway and what if I should find myself feeling unhappy right in the middle of some gay song?

I've met E. again and on the very shores where we first met five years ago and fell in love (sailboats in the distance, middle ground, and foreground). He hasn't changed since my last letter. I mention flute players to him only in passing. I believe I have never been more logical than I am at this moment, 12 o'clock, Eastern Standard Time, the sun bouncing off my watch crystal and into his eyes. I have nothing to regret as yet, but I am plagued by an ever-present sense of *déjà vu.* It seems to me that we sat in a bar like this one at some other 12 o'clock with sirens down the street. Once I had a black purse just like this. Once, winding my Timex, I looked toward the reflection of the sun, wondering if I should offer to pay for my own drink. I could have heard the waves from here if I tried.

This is more than a question of preference. One makes choices on a deeper level than that. I judge the tilt of the cherry in my glass. The stem points to the door. On the other hand, the cherry itself lies with a wrinkle on the top that seems to be looking out the window (as he is). But I feel I have made this judgment once before. I chose the window which looks out onto the sea.

Sometimes I imagine myself with a knife in my back, chest crushed by the steering post, my hand in the blender, my foot on the third rail, drowning in a surf too strong for me. Perhaps it's lack of sleep that brings on such thoughts, but that's why I'm not listening to the sea now.

I sense the high point of the afternoon coming soon after the third cocktail, after he says, "I still love you," et cetera. I suppose it's always best not to argue too much. I'm agreeable but I'm not planning on losing any sleep. If depression should, in any case, result, I have a little pill that will restore the sense of well-being. (Now I lay me down to love.) In a dream I have seen two fish fly by. Will I meet him again on some other beach, I wonder? and will I think it has all happened sometime before?

But things go along about as well as could be expected and I will keep on with the diary of lost sleep just so long as nobody goes mad or dies or has a baby and if I don't cut my finger off whipping the cream.

THE VOICE BEHIND THE CURTAIN

GOTTFRIED BENN

Translated by David Harris

I: THE EXAMPLES

ALFRED. Fade behind the curtain, great Father, it is better that people don't look each other in the eye. There, you can draw on your pipe or stroke your beard, even take a nap if it bores you; and I personally like talking to a wall, it's a natural listener. If you want people to notice you're there, just ring the bell. I've set up two bells with different tones. The lighter one means: more quickly, not so many details; the other one means: more slowly, greater depth. If you ring both of them it means: you're touching upon the cosmic, don't go all the way. I'll begin—Selah.

I am Alfred, your firstborn son. You named us according to the alphabet. Berthold isn't here yet, he's coming later. He doesn't yet know what he should recite, what's on his mind, everything's confused. The program is entitled: what does the procreator say to his sons and daughters these days. The years of procreation lie thirty years to sixty years in the past. It will be polished up to a certain extent, but they're not supposed to be talking a lot of nonsense anyway. Personally, I find myself in such a state that I have no desire anymore to express what I could or might like to express. It's a compromise from the very beginning. So, either the thing goes on by itself and then it's not necessary to speak, or somebody has to give it a push, and I don't want to be the one to do that. If there is something holy in everything, then we must look for it. If there are great commandments, then we must ask ourselves what we think of them. If there are calls from distant worlds then we must try to listen for them—"must" and "distant worlds"—is that the tempter speaking already?

At the moment I am occupied with slips in happy marriages. Loyalty is such a tremendous inner process that one can neither teach nor preach it. In practice, my motto is: good direction is better than loyalty. Protect the partner, don't let him notice, no fanaticism for reality in these things. But if you lose control . . . Oh, here comes Cilly, "C" as in Cherie, or rather number three. Cilly, can a woman love two men?

CILLY. Certainly she can.

ALFRED. But if she really loves the first one, melts together with him, wax in his hands, can she still love the second one?

CILLY. Certainly she can.

ALFRED. How does she do it?

CILLY. Maybe one is old and the other's young, maybe he's a god and the other's a man. She'll always feel tremendously flattered if the god begets her, but she'll always go with the other one. It's impossible for a man to count on love, if he doesn't have a certain amount of banality; above all he has to be around all the time, and the gods have so many directorial commitments—God only knows where.

ALFRED. If there's something holy in everything, then it must be in sensuality too.

CILLY. Can you imagine a sensuous buyer or congressman. The word comes from the age of Aphrodite.

THE VOICE. None of this historicism. Concrete examples!

EXAMPLE I. I'm the man past sixty, do you think I am going to let my wife wither my last months? A nice person, but this is a question of extension. When the end comes, then you've got to crawl into the gutter, you don't fall far anymore. What can happen to you after that? Divorce? Delirium? Puerperal fever is out of the question—death is such an infamous thing that, he who dares to offer you that as the abundance of the last beats, has a crooked baton.

ALFRED. Perfectly correct, what the man says. What do you think, Cilly?

CILLY. Listen a little more.

EXAMPLE I. And with what sort of people did you spend these sixty years? Just go through the streets, what a bunch of apes. The restaurant owners stand in front of their doors and hope that all the passersby are hungry and thirsty, the dentists that their teeth are rotting, the shoe manufacturers that their shoes will split, the priests that hell will become more apparent, the lawyers are crying for murder—they're all screaming for roles, big leading ones with lots of success and laurels. None of them can simply say: You can all kiss my . . . or as Tao says it: Act through your being. But none of them are negative individuals; more likely they're compromising, nature-lovers, all longing for the Königssee with steep rocky cliffs.

CILLY. There's something to that.

EXAMPLE I. That's the kind you've spent the years with. Faces, faces! I see a man going into a bar, he has a wonderful *cache-nez* scarf, stitched gloves, takes everything off so carefully, smoothes out everything so nicely on the hanger as if it were a significant thing. He sits there so pleased with himself, you'd think the moon rose just for him. The whole thing's a conglomerate—rip out the teeth, rip out the tonsils, rip out the appendix, rip out the womb, the shaped form that dismembers itself prophylactically. And at the next table how happy the man is when his friend pinches his wife's knee—a sort of confirmation. As far as I'm concerned, they're all junk thieves, bums, they go to the toilet, toss the *pissoirs* into their rucksacks—booze down their gullets, stinking livers, sugar in their urinal tracts—but the pious man who rounds off everything—hail to him. For a meaningful experience do we want the pious man? No, he's only the limited one.

THE VOICE. Wait and see!

EXAMPLE I. So these beings have faces, they wear them out front, through the grounds, in the parlor, on trips—it's all a big front. Greedy, ripped apart, gray from failure and need; and then they know of a face they want to have near them, a face they want to drink, a special face, a certain face—do you think I would let myself be stopped from going to it? If there's something holy in everything . . .

BERTHOLD. I was listening to the last of that. How would it be if you talked to your wife? Maybe she isn't as limited as you think . . .

EXAMPLE I. I'm afraid that would make the whole thing lose its tension.

CILLY. But, just between us, you know, you have a face too . . .

BERTHOLD. Isn't what's holy merely an abstraction with bass organ tones?

THE VOICE. That comes later. Your examples, Berthold!

EXAMPLE II. I live on my Social Security—it's not much, but enough for the pleasant life of an idler. If the day begins with rain, you can stay at home. If it begins with sunshine, you can sit on a park bench. Old? Sure, but let the others die off first, there's enough of them around. I must have accomplished something, they're treating me so well. Forgotten? Now you go from day to day, looking at this and that and ask yourself: What is man's goal? Is it trips like Ulysses'—seven years with Calypso, Circe lying in a hammock, looking into Nausicaä's eyes. Or trudging about in the polar regions like Nansen? Or fifty years at the office with the rules of the old school: regular vacations and a steady salary? Yesterday I got a prescription for arches for my shoes—it's not that I couldn't walk without them, but the running around does pass the time.

EXAMPLE III. I run a little "salon"—you know what I mean—it's not that I'm immoral, but the gentlemen do have certain wishes, sometimes I really have my hands full and by evening I'm dripping like a rag. It's essentially a morning business—a skip and a jump from the office or the delivery truck. Please park a little way off! Most of them are easy to handle, but every once in a while we get one who wants the naughty student bit, complete with kneeboots and switches. Courage, ladies! Some of the gentlemen like sophisticated conversation as an appetizer—the sort of talk you'd hear at Merano—but my philosophy is: it's all right if a girl is smart, but if she isn't, it has as little significance as hoarseness does for a violinist. My young ladies aren't dissatisfied, but once in a while they grumble about the runs in their stockings; some of the cavaliers don't have very smooth hands. Four pairs of nylons a week is certainly something you can't take as a tax deduction. Some of the gentlemen come at eight in the morning, it probably has to do with their business constellations, so we see the ups and downs of trade and industry.

EXAMPLE IV. I'm a landlord, but don't mind that. Managed to

bring a rooming house through the war safely and the same with another elegant house and grounds, sold the latter at a good profit. Stupid tenants. They sat in the cellar, but kept lookouts and put out the fire from the bombs. I was holed up in a much safer place. And now the bastards want hot water, even the subtenants, suit them just fine to wash themselves under streams of heat, why I'd have to repair the pipes—and my new country house in Düsseldorf. In the room where I receive my clients, a beaten-up armchair, take a seat, careful, there, do you see how I sacrifice so much for you. But if they get smart, if it rains through and so forth—stand up! He's never made the fearful happy, old God. Every evening I pray in honor of Dehmel: give it to me, give it to me—a raise in my rents.

THE VOICE. Very nice types—but all somewhat limited. The freest of them was the one on Social Security. I want to look that up about Circe in her hammock.

ALFRED. And holiness is in all things. Have to make a note of that. Everything, that has existed: pyramids, martyrs, cathedrals, preludes, it's in them, too. Does that rhyme? There must be a vast interconnection somewhere. For a while everything is over and after a while everything is there again. You can't stop and you can't begin. Things begin differently in the summer than in the winter. In the summer something intense creeps through all the cracks, more so than in the winter. But we have a sack over our heads and just keep on feeling our way forward.

BERTHOLD. But we know too little. I first learned something about mousetraps when I was fifty. They have to be handled differently. With field mice, which are very sensitive to the presence of man, you must boil the trap after it's caught one, whereas the simple domestic mouse and the pack rat, being tamed animals, don't require such special treatment. There is a tremendous amount of experience among men and mice, observations, comparisons, measures and instincts, a world of its own, and all of this was foreign to me.

DONATH. It's the same way with things of an inner nature. Have you ever seen a weak person, someone you would hardly notice, suddenly become strong and powerful before your very eyes? You come into contact with a waitress, waiting on customers, a subordinate personality, crises arise, differences, two-facedness. And suddenly you receive a certain warmth, a certain current from the simple hand that waits on tables and carries china around, and you come a little further.

ALFRED. And this expansion of tender things. In 1738, the camellia was introduced from Japan—what a springtime. A flower was introduced. And now everybody knows the camellia lady, *La Dame aux Camélias*—arias of mourning, heartrending syncopes. Sometimes I sink into camellias, into their name, in the south out in the open, the plant in a vase you don't dare touch, suddenly the blossom falls, crashes to the ground, you hear it—the dream is gone —I collapse.

THE VOICE. Tender, tenderer, tenderest. No soft spots!

EXAMPLE I. Speaking of myself once more, everything wasted, no power left, but to see this face I mentioned sink again, she closes her eyes, hurling its innermost feelings from itself, glowing and familiar, and nearby the warmth and the clarity and the happiness. Perhaps you love your wife, but, when you're with the other one you're completely enchanted by her, and when you're alone you don't think about either of them. The one is like your vest and the other is like your tie and you certainly can't go naked . . .

EXAMPLE III. Perhaps, in all modesty, I can be of service. Tell me your type, the mood of this face, its characteristics and features, strawberry blond or salt and pepper, and the neck, the neck . . .

EXAMPLE II. You're touching on a singular problem there. It's not the body, the spirit even less, one of my greatest infatuations had never heard Nietzsche's name before and I have a brain like a spade, I furrow. I've seen the most beautiful, the most intelligent, the most enchanting, women, and yet I never stayed with them until the end. But in this connection even things of lesser importance achieve a different meaning. What is this whole thing then? An attack, an incident, a coincidence . . .

EXAMPLE III. An accident.

EXAMPLE I. Then there ought to be some sort of insurance against that.

EXAMPLE III. My house is an insurance and at reasonable prices.

ALFRED, DONATH, BERTHOLD. And now let us sing the aria.

ALFRED. To be as it was in the old times once more: irresponsible and not to know the end, to feel the flesh: thirst, tenderness, conquering, losing, to reach over into that other thing—into what? To sit here in the evening, to look into the abyss of the night, it narrows, but there are flowers at the base of it, the scent rises, short and trembling, behind it, of course, the putrefaction, then everything is dark and you know your part again, you throw down your money and leave . . .

BERTHOLD. Early in the morning there are hydrangeas in front of the bathroom, pink heads, an extremely silent flower, it is the aurora that greets me in them. Sometimes there was even a melody out of one of the houses, sometimes very orgiastic, those were the summers. It seems irresponsible to me now that something like that exists, which others saw too and will see, later on and long ago, and again and again forever—a person ought never to see such irretrievable things.

DONATH. Or it is tropical, the air moistens your skin, the drinks dampen your tissues. This atmosphere! It always makes me think of primordial times, of fern leaves and the formations of strata. On the other hand, at the table next to me, the salad plates and Coca-Cola push their way into my eye—thus life complements itself and makes an attempt at totality. But, again and again, you glide forever backward and forward from all things into an impersonal distance. The momentary—and not being able to hold anything, look around and everything moves on. You love a woman, you are with her, you really love her, there's nothing but the two of you, no world, only the night and the words between you, these words from God knows where, the first words as if from Eden, the last words which bind as well as destroy—I said there is no world there, only the two of you—but there, where the pillow ends, what hits you there in the eye? I'm asking you, I don't want to say anything . . .

(Both bells ring.)

ALFRED, BERTHOLD, DONATH. Why so cosmic? I don't understand.

THE VOICE. Sorry, I had fallen asleep and dropped them on the ground.

ALFRED. You are looking through a balcony door over geraniums into the night. Now it expands in front of your penetrating stare: at the top, the white nights of Stockholm, in Seville, they dance the fandango, a rose in their hair; in Charleston, the ladies and gentlemen throw their cigarettes into the hibiscus pots and stream back into the auditorium. Everything as always, no change in the widths, how many long things there are, only with you it's certain that you won't be blowing the smoke through your nose without limit.

BERTHOLD. With reduced means, without nature, you live in a part of the city, desolate on summer Sundays. But then if you have to admit to yourself that there will only be a few more even of these summer Sundays, a pressure arises. Then you drive up to one of the beautiful lakes, overcrowded, but water and sails and vapor, the skin goes into flame, the wind brushes your parts, strange being, it is the other thing, nature, and the brown legs of female lackadaisicality in beach chairs and wicker cabins distracting you, beautiful hours, free and fatiguing, but, just the same, hours—and yet the whole thing, what do you take hold of there?

DONATH. Or you sweep past a café terrace, every chair is taken. The faces of the ladies surrender to the night, to the man, to love, the men's appearance is smooth and impressive. Soft are these faces of the ladies, pained, sweet, and bowed toward destiny. Thus pass the nights. Faithfulness, love, readiness for pain, arising out of the one great feeling—then it collapses, be it because of the transitoriness of time or of early deceit.

CILLY. You're all stupid. Let's talk about my brown dress, can I still wear the coat or does the skirt show—and then the new muffs, everything else will resolve itself, we don't cause any trouble.

ALFRED. Much is too beautiful to look at and much is too little to interpret—there is a painful dilemma between gaze and chimera.

BERTHOLD. Or the moon stands awkwardly in the sky, withering away, but still big. Over all the streets its huge oval, it reminds you of storms, withering, of ending and darkened hours. There, you would like to help and bring happiness, but you injure something within yourself which seeks intoxication and personal ecstasy, form and perfection. Forced to a word of pity at the wrong time for another person, you destroy everything, and the emptiness is there again—that incomprehensible weakness toward everything, that world of benevolence on the one hand and on the other something that desires to remain untouched. Great Father, say a word.

THE VOICE. What's supposed to happen?

DONATH. Or certain autumn evenings, mist and behind it a little yellow-gold, a bridge vanishes and cloaks its arches. Step back, says the one voice, expand yourself for the losses—keep yourself, says the other one, cast your gathering gaze over everything.

EXAMPLE I. Let me sing with you. There is a dance floor, on it a tender pair, their feet move in conformity, in the middle they wriggle about one another, at the top synthesis has taken place, he sings the words into her mouth too, the mouth has white teeth, he lets her dance through his arms—that is sweeter than an orgasm.

EXAMPLE III. If that's not sensual . . .

BERTHOLD. Example I, what is your profession?

EXAMPLE I. Fruit dealer—sour grapes and road apples.

THE VOICE. The great entanglement—that's how it should be.

II: THE SUNDAY PAPER

EMIL. Great Father, I bring you the Sunday paper, the day of the Lord is taken care of when you've gotten through it; it furnishes man and animal and green vegetation, it contains all of his works, the Sunday papers are enormous! They inform you about the little and the big light, the fog that moistens the land, the waters of the lands of the Moors and the waters of the Hiddekel, they represent the Tree of Life and the Tree of Knowledge, they do justice to the seven days of creation in only thirty-six pages.

We need the contents of the paper if we want to go on, the desire of form does not regenerate itself just by productivity, it requires material. For many years the artist lives evenly, indifferently, lives on quietly and draws from his resources. But then only shocks can bring him further, impressions, vast knowledge and reports—here they are, in generous proportions, instructive and pleasing—may he reach into the grab bag and enrich himself with details and be in command of his faces.

Let's start with page one! Here you get the feeling that man is so constructed that everything goes wrong with him: he can't prevent the wars, he can't introduce any just social order, and when he begins to think, it becomes tragic.

CILLY. Page one without me. Can't you begin with the women's section? Last Sunday, there was something about Charlotte Buff, marriage among petty officials, and now an abandoned grave, very painful, don't you have anything like that?

EMIL. Popular colors in Paris, 1792: the color of old fleas, the color of flies' backs, the color of dirty Paris streets—all that is coming, Cilly, be patient. All right, page one. Once again, various diplomatic notes have been exchanged and various councils have had general assemblies. It has to be this way of course. The significance of certain channels of water is indubitable and history demands it.

THE VOICE. Emil, I consider your attitude completely out of place. The masses are always right, the press is always right; who will read the ads if something like that isn't said first? Plus which the man of today has just as valid a need for opinions and points of view as the man of yesterday did for rites; the exchange of news is the present cosmos of the white earth.

EMIL. Exactly, Papa, now let's turn to page 3 for the conventions. The topic for the meeting was "The Cruelty of Fairy Tales." The speaker reported on the terrifying statistics of *Grimm's Fairy Tales,* based on true instances of cruelty, and demanded their elimination. Mrs. K., probably the most important expert today on fairy tale literature, was able to give interpretations that threw light on the problem from a historical-psychological point of view. The child's deep fear of the stepmother and the boogeyman.

CILLY. Do you know anything about that? I can't remember anything.

EMIL. Shut your mouth, these are experts talking. It goes on: "The attending psychologists, Professor T. and Lecturer Dr. Z., pointed out the element of irreality."

CILLY. What do they mean by "irreal?" I think they want to cure something here.

EMIL. But there are also happy reports, even happy announcements, even happy hopes—the Federal Railways and the PEN Club are at work and they are certainly forces to reckon with. "Snow White" was the cruelest of them all, even Ortega y Gasset has commented on her. There was no discussion of the *Iliad* or Heine's "Three Grenadiers." However, one of the speakers did point out the pedagogically questionable aspect of barking deer and was applauded for warning against forest walks in October.

THE VOICE. How were the flower arrangements?

EMIL. Only corn blossoms and alpine orchids. At the banquet somebody praised the advantages of *raw* vegetables and was severely chastised; Red Ridinghood Sec and Henkell Brut champagne were prohibited.

THE VOICE. We are here obviously confronted with the problem of prophylaxis. Prophylactics from whom, against what, from what position, in what direction. Here we approach a crisis.

EMIL. But first the ads! I love the ads for the little man.

CILLY. We're all little people.

EMIL. I need a magnifying glass for that. "Wherever I go, I always have my Knak watch with me."—that's an allusion to Loewe; Loewe's ballads, that assumes a great deal. "Deer antlers, rack of venison, rhinoceros, elephants' teeth"—the tropics at the doorstep. "Cock-a-doodle-do, hen and cock look for old china, china specialties with plastic blossoms—" We don't need to go to the salons, business and industry speak here too. We are a fantastic nation. What is elegant comes from foreign countries, what is attractive, from overseas. We don't even exist anymore, but the ads are cultivated.

DONATH. Eleven o'clock and still no second breakfast. You don't need to read any more for me. One paper is just like another. We know all that anyway. The sensations during the act and the sensations during the flight, the lights of Paris and the prefabricated houses at the edge of the salty desert, grouping of past events and perspectives for the year 2000, we know all that off the cuff, it's a big card catalog where everything is listed.

BERTHOLD. Agreed! But talking is even worse. Talking, laughing, waving your cigar, the ladies have such elegant movements too —that may be all right for a small table. But from a broader point of view, youth can hardly talk with its elders anymore; there, there is impulse, here, there is experience, and when the flesh becomes less impulsive we get different results. The religious person can't talk to the worldly one who never received the gift of religion, he thinks along a plane and linearly. The mother can't talk to her daughter, because the daughter hides her pleasures and her shame. The artist can't talk to the politician, one is outside of time and the other lives in the present. The industrialist talks of refrigerators and the danger of surplus exports—who listens to that? A gentleman was in Arosa—snowfall from Thursday to Monday: "I must honestly say, that was too much"—whether honest or dishonest, why the ethical considerations, he simply has to accept that kind of bad weather if he dares to reach those heights. In short: why all of these juxtapositions, we certainly know, everything is antinomic—or I've been invited to visit somebody whose address is "In the Black Valley," that sounds like morass, wild boars and long treks, and afterward we're supposed to talk together, how can he expect that of me, I don't have any sandals for that.

ALFRED. Tohowabohu, but nobody wants to know it, a large assessment, but nobody wants to pay it. Twilight, in the blue rippling of the evening, the hour whitens, neither owl nor lark, neither bat nor cock. Zigzag. From a hotel window I looked at the high trees. A lucky coincidence had led me to this house. Barcarole—treetops, underneath the Canadian quince, which a sea captain introduced here a hundred years ago, blue waves and stars and the night rushing in. I thought of my sins. What is the measure for sins? On my table lay a Sunday newspaper with the words Goethe had written when he was eighty: "Happiness requires courage, have this courage!" Neither mourning, nor refusal, nor asceticism requires courage—but happiness! But does the old man say what happiness is? My happinesses, to be precise, were all connected with crimes: adultery, intoxication, disloyalty, hating my parents, deceit, double morals, and even Hamsun's words occurred to me: "There is only one love, the stolen one"—one of the great truths in the history of man—could Goethe have recommended that? But do we ever know what we mean—did he mean anything at all? I threw the paper down in annoyance; for myself, I only know that my brain has been stretched across an unbelievably hard surface all my life, and now it transmits super-destructive cartridges—or does anyone else sense how close the substance, the fecundity, and the innerness are to the deadened senses—actually only the crime continues.

THE VOICE. The crisis!

EMIL. Here's something for you, Cilly, from the society column, interesting, it sounds like a modern ballad. As I said before, the artist finds material here in the paper too—it goes like this:

Little old lady
in a big red room
little old lady—
hums Marion Davies,

while Hearst, her friend for thirty years,
in a heavy copper casket under the protection
of a strong
escort
and followed by twenty-two limousines
arrives before the marble mausoleum,
the television cameras buzz softly.

Little old lady, big red room,
henna red, soft gladiola red, emperor red
(purple snail).
Bedroom in Santa Monica castle
à la Pompadour

Louella, she calls, radio!
The Blues, Jitterbug—zigzag!
Society in the Atlantic region:
eligible daughters and obliterated sexus,
Palazzos along the bays, feather blankets on soft beds.
they separate the world into monde and demimonde—
I was always the latter—

Louella, my mixture—high proof!
What is all this?
discouraged, fought up, suffered like dogs—
the lines, ugly lines, which the copper casket
now cancels,
a light shone when he saw me,
the rich love too, tremble, and know damnation.

High proof—the glass on the silver service,
he will now be silent at that hour,
which we only knew—
funny sayings came out of the earpiece,
"life decides in breakfast nooks,
on the beach it hails granite from bathing suits,
always the unexpected,
the hoped-for never happens"—
those were his stories.

The promenade's over! Only a few stone tiles still,
the glass on the foremost
high proof, shattering, last rhapsody—
little old lady,
in a big red room.

CILLY. And do you know how it ended? The family shipped her off, after ten days the will was opened and she was sole heir. Six weeks later she married an elegant American naval officer.

EMIL. But then I didn't need to be so poetic. Great Father, that is certainly a change in life.

THE VOICE. What's supposed to happen?

FERDINAND. Page five first. There's something weird about these papers. Take them away! It's all worlds you've never seen. Rooms of cloud-red stones; landscapes with little motion in them, some smoke from a ranch, a beady-eyed bird. The cellophane-thin skin of a snake lies peeled off across the path, large stagnating ponds, above them motionless butterflies. Wildcats, drunken with the sap of deadly nightshade, scream, howl, reel—where are you looking? At things you never were, never will be, you can't reach them—worlds of such things—unbearable!

EMIL. And outside the attack on the tropics begins. West Africa in the lead, but Nigeria too. Here, in the business section: "Nigeria seeks felt hats." Where eight hundred thousand once lived, now ten billion can be nourished—an influx! But who rushes there—you maybe? Eventful environment! New South Wales has its coldest day in seventy-nine years—snow in Canberra; short-lived army revolts in Honduras—and you? You know the turn of the daily order that passes up something of no consequence. The Indian zoo has been offered a giant salamander as a token of friendship from Nippon, science reports hope in saving eyes infested with cystic worms—and you? Let's simply admit it: only a track is present! And where does the track lead to? Into last year's snow.

GERHARD. Yes, take the paper away, that's too bitter. Floods of incapacity and failure cover the heart, floods of yearning and November, floods of Land's End and Finisterre. Asia, Africa, Honolulu, smother your flame—granite, masses, iceflows, Tulip Islands run over you with fresh sensations, you are lost, do you have the bodily strength to reach them—do you have the money? I shall now practice a little radarthinking and demonstrate.

EXAMPLE V. I am the radarthinker. Here, there is no material obtrusiveness, I am taking a bearing. The man at the window, the follower of a train of thought in his own home. Looking at the street, focusing on certain details, but immediately back to the attic. I create my own causality, I keep my head free, there must always be hollow space in there for the formations. My apparatus works methodically: it keeps going back to itself, holds itself by the gums, tastes itself on the tongue, its own paprika, picks the jewels itself, a lot of the thing in itself and a pinch of the saeculum-hey, that's the radarthinker.

My principles are as follows: avoid distances, avoid abundance, for if you read all of that, the question always arises: if it hadn't come to that: splitting of the atom, dynamite, insulin, sweetened lupine—what then, how would things be then, but then in the first place supposedly something new would have been added, or in the second place nothing new would have been added, but would that have changed anything in the principles of the world? No, avoid distances, avoid continuity, couple yourself with your inner resources—take bearings, take soundings, stock up, but then back to the formations immediately. Read the newspaper, but sublimate the matrices. From the shadows look out at the glowing trees and flowers—this Japanese garden principle—that's what my window offers you. Stay in the shadows, keep to yourself, the world keeps to itself.

HERWARTH. Obviously a relative of Example II, on a pension. We won't get any further with that. This old character is antiquated. Odol, aspirin, Pyramidon, how it all comes to life, because so many people use it. Anachronistic this hollow space. Our grandparents could radarthink, there were wonderful positions: trustee, tricky contracts, and new issues, or specialist for ear, nose, and throat, paint the throat a bit and they won't call you at night—salesmen for Suchard chocolate, very much in demand, you only needed to pick up the receiver and note down the orders, today, you've got to keep your nose to the grindstone day and night, finance bums, knock on doors, twist and turn, slippery and threatening, track down advertisements, deftly wagging your tail, study the boss's tone of voice when he leaves the office in the evening: "anything else?"

ISAAC. All in all, Sunday's half over and everywhere nothing but precarious situations. A swarm of thoughts, theses, aspirations, and no answer. You think you'll find an answer in every Sunday issue, an Ave Maria, a liturgy, but always it's only those punctuation marks and nothing further. You read the newspaper from beginning to end, even the small print, and then you go out into the day and if you want to win anything, you must go at it with your most naked heart.

Sometimes I think, the creator said to himself, they only need five fingers and that's enough, and in general he was right—so maybe we have these five fingers on the inside too, but we don't, this organization has only wings and fins, the devices of motion in uncertain media. Only the flesh sets itself in motion with all certainty. But the whole thing including spirit and style and customs—what does it amount to?

THE VOICE. What's it supposed to be?

ISAAC. Great Father, can't we look up from the paper anymore and ask something general, can't we ever ask how things really stand with the creator? For example, he was very successful with the murderous elements and the bloodthirstiness among tigers and leopards, but inside of us too, there are things that aren't the way they ought to be and the way we want them to be. You know what it's like when a person's heart is broken. Most of the time it isn't you at all, but someone else, whom you destroyed, a good person, a believer, from whom you took everything. Sure, you can say, belief is at fault, you always have to count on the worst in every situation, but then why all the songs that sound so sweet on the accordion or the guitar—there must be something besides the worst. You read all the newspapers from front to back, you constantly subscribe to new ones, but you don't get any further, you've got a sack over your head, you flail your arms, turn to the creator, you pray to G——.

THE VOICE. Leave G—— out of this. Just because you've worn your rubber soles out doesn't make him a cobbler.

ISAAC. No, it doesn't, but you think about him more often. Soon the hour will come when you'll have to put your face into the darkness, into the big black sponge, and then the shadows will fall upon you and out of the shadows you can make nothing good again and atone for nothing. You live in what people saw of you and knew of you up to then—see obituary notice—shouldn't we live like that before the shadows fall?

THE VOICE. Get thee to a nunnery, Ophelia.

ALFRED. But, Great Father, now there are pine boughs on all the pianos again, and catkins too, ahead of time, read the articles of advent, the seasons and the Christian holidays rush about us —again and again—but then, Great Father, what happens then—say something.

THE VOICE. What's wrong with that?

BERTHOLD. And the records, the new hits: the port of Adano and Dolores's legs fly about in your head, a maelstrom of current beauties, unsteady sweet moods, this year and another year, and then, Great Father, what happens then?

THE VOICE. (*threatening*) What's wrong with that?

KATJA. You leave one for another, good, one is young and the other is old, you believe in each of them. "As a God, everyone has walked" (*Ariadne,* Strauss), but when he leaves, you are alone and read the marriage announcements and the wrinkles come, the sleepless nights, the menopause—what's holy then—what happens then?

THE VOICE. (*shouting*) What's supposed to happen, who are you then, created and developed, eyes filled with tears and hearts rocking back and forth. Swallow your guts for once and your legs and shut up about your tripe, or as the psalmist says: my soul is still before God. What's wrong, what you call holy, I call foolish, your wishy-washy little worries full of sentimentality and bladder panic —off to potty quickly every time! If you could feel what an aeon is—but how could you ever feel that anyway? You intellectual chimpanzees, go right on with your close-out sale—pensioners, whores, landlords, all a bunch of tramps in the park, whinnying in the balcony if hearts are dying on the stage—what's supposed to happen, how many nights have you stood alone, which sadness have you carried silently—the nothingness, your nothingness was always spotted with prayer counters and shoestrings—if I said to you now: live in the darkness, do in the darkness what we can—*that's what's supposed to happen?* But what am I getting excited for? You say I created you? That's looking at things too personally and too mechanistically, I certainly didn't think of you when I went with your mother, I thought about something completely different, her face was always so beautiful when we made love. Children are strange people, you have to go back to older things than me, if you're going to speak of creation.

Here are your bells back, that's another one of those intellectual farces. *(The Voice throws the bells over the curtain.)* I want to smear my beard with something completely different, I want to see a garden in the summer and want to see how the snow falls and nothing else.

(All sing from the Sunday newspaper.)

A strange old current undulates,
sometimes white and sometimes blue Nile,
and 'neath the skin it circulates,
playing in thought and love the while.

Much inherited, something won,
old fountain, something new was found,
and our father is now long gone,
yet he produced us, still and sound.

Into the big woods he has fled,
into the bushes, darkest green,
through the underbrush he has sped,
we praise him, manly and serene.

III: MELANCHOLY AND NEON LIGHTING

EXAMPLE I. Two months later. We have all matured morally and spiritually. I have disassociated myself from the face I wanted to drink; I have told her to stay with her friend, the one with whom she deceived me, a greengrocer. I called, her voice sounded so strange; I just got out of the bath she said, I knew what was up. Take your false teeth out, I screamed, show the man that you only have two teeth left in your upper jaw, I loved you just the same, I'm not so sure about him—that made her mad. I'll stick to my wife, a wonderful person, my secure port for starting on new adventures—zigzag. In Neukölln there's a bar with table telephones and a pneumatic post system, I think I'll make a trek out there today.

CHOIR. That is the will to live, the intractable one.

EXAMPLE IV. The rent increase has been rejected, but since I refuse them hot water I save on that, for six years now, by the way, not one of the dopes has noticed it, it's certainly a legitimate cause for complaint. My new house in Düsseldorf is a little small, I have to lay three rugs one on top of another, but then nobody knows what I really have there. Sure there'll be complaints and trouble-makers there too, the world is seething with people wanting to rent a room. I've told the manager here to do absolutely nothing for them, he's to annoy them till they piss oil, no elevator, no glass for the windows, no shingles on the roof—this civilization is laughable for such room grubs, the apartments are wonderful compared to doghouses. So long, don't take any wooden nickels.

CHOIR. That's a head for business, that's what builds up the country.

EXAMPLE II. In the meantime I've had twelve ultra-sound vibration treatments, you've got to keep up with the times.

CHOIR. That's the evening of life in the shadow of the oak of welfare.

EXAMPLE III. The police were wonderful, stayed in the front room until I could remove the tools from the back rooms, whips, lashes, ropes, and straps. In the end, they said, madam, your apartment only has three rooms and you have five little doves as tenants, where do the five ladies dream after the day's labor and toil? In seventh heaven, I said, and the gentlemen laughed. The women's clubs are on the warpath against sensuality, but those were wonderful executives.

CHOIR. That is love in all of its variations, of which Aeschylus's choir once said, "O Eros, thou never in battle conquered."

CHOIR LEADER. Those are a few examples, but aren't they beautiful! Is all that aimed at the *deep* person? Who is a deep person? Was Socrates a deep person? According to the State he seduced youth and died happy. Alexander, Mohammed, Eisenhower—is the elementary deep or the sublime, is good deep or crime? If there had only been martyrs and penitents, where would we be? And if we all kept silent? No Great Father any more to counsel us!

"So sink, then, one can say, too, climb" (*Faust*)—what's that supposed to mean? Obviously, there are considerations that are both positive and negative. Someplace it flames up, and someplace it dies out, somewhere a nova, and somewhere another grain of dust among the ashes of the world. Where do we stand, at what point among the fauna, through which flora do we wind our way? Much seems to say, it is a dream of autumn, the roses tip their glass: empty, a last drop on its misty side, the gardens whisper brown and pale violet, transparent into the flat distance.

So these roses sink, but from "E2" apartments, built on columns with arcades for shops, baths and restaurants and even a hotel for houseguests, we will look out at the new lilacs. Why do we still ask, what's supposed to happen, we've got to get to the end. One more word on our geographic situation. You could say we're local bigshots, sealed-off island niggers, stormtroopers—no, all over Europe it's the same thing. A diplomat from the most secure country in the world, not a German, internationally known, asserted the following: "Already, the clearest symptom of the complete and catastrophic evolution of our age had reached that stage where all words and all names had lost their meaning, the symbol which the spirit had created in architecture and in works of music is no longer true, everything's a lie, everything is fading and will be suddenly extinguished and will disappear completely." Fantastic words! The words of a diplomat. From a famous family of the old style, the Continental atmosphere of golf etiquette, the best of Europe in the old hierarchical tradition, and he speaks in detail of the last stage of our age. No, we're not local bigshots, no special city-states, it extends over the whole continent, it has broken its yoke and burst its bonds. Thus everything flows together, blood, saliva, tears, sperm, who's to say what is right and what is important?

We blew in all four directions, the weather vane is much too small. The great intermingling, holiness in everything. Forever and again accept your fate, mourning and light, melancholy and neon lighting, arrogance, fornication, exploitation, and then the high things: the cup of hemlock and the thorns on the cross. Before whom shall we kneel now? The old one has left us in a rut, the situation is bad. Forever and again, accept your fate—you, examples and speakers, before whom can we kneel now? At the most, before his strange words: "Live in the darkness, do what we can in the darkness." But what is that supposed to mean?

THE END

This short play carried the following dedication:

Dedicated to my wife,
a generation younger than I
who, with gentle and sagacious hands,
arranged the hours and the steps
and the asters in the vases.

THIRTEEN POEMS

ED ROBERSON

true we are two grown men

true we are two grown men
beyond the wand-length of magical things
and sting of crazy-berry thorns.
but this bend is what we turn lately back into. where
the trains S close to the river
where we mad used to play.
out after school has been these years.
for you, a wife; for me, the want
of what we always came
here for anyhow, come now
again hunting to commit
before our each weak end-outrage.

coming on behind the clock work
of their engines march the cars
like minutes to throw life at.
we watch the thing throw up the spark
that stones do round about sunset

true we are two grown men
for whom time's wild caboose too soon
will wave away our chance to lay

our heads our wooden eyes
spite-wide upon the railroad tie
and watch the thunderous universe
of will pass so near over us
coach after raging coach.

the resignation of madame chairman succubus

how many companies
of flavor strawberries
become along the vine
of distribution   love

i do not know. and time
has brought a tasteless kind
of buyer who above
his knees and chin has been

disorganized. my glove
of blood for picking love
off stems of men
goes pressureless from dealing

and won't hold. i tend
toward like most women
the tongue's investing
taste for husbandry.

directions to the party

streetcar him to the one part of the city
too fast to bed these tracks or even lightning's,
the section thunder took a loss and moved
out of and rain won't go into without protection.
streetcar him in a car that has the smell
of other lips' lipstick squirting the name
and locale of the product through the shattered paint,

of users fallen forward then yanked back
at stops and starts to show their open dead eyes
    and the bruises on their heads from going home.
    his is the stop where fire out of control
brings those who don't believe the burning know
the stiffness of the flame and how its feet
stand stupidly before them while they demonstrate the dance.

poem

it has scratched shadows
angels that meant its passing   on my gate
it has bent down my stalk of sun
until the bloom breaks off behind the hill
it has stuck wads of breath into
a toy man sickness had played with
one game after another
and it has looked in one man's eye
and was not seen to walk away

what has gone on with it behind the doors
that, closed off, define me in this building
i am jealous of
and print upon the door
                                        a hall is spent
taking what we are called between us yet

its boot crossing the same field
            has brought to mud
the hard earth finally
a day nothing can get through but that it enters

sonnet

i must be careful about such things as these.
the thin-grained oak. the quiet grizzlies scared
into the hills by the constant tracks squeezing

in behind them closer in the snow. the snared
rigidity of the winter lake. deer after deer
crossing on the spines of fish who look up and stare
with their eyes pressed to the ice. in a sleep. hearing
the thin taps leading away to collapse like the bear
in the high quiet. i must be careful not to shake
anything in too wild an elation. not to jar
the fragile mountains against the paper far-
ness. nor avalanche the fog or the eagle from the air.
of the gentle wilderness i must set the precarious
words. like rocks. without one snowcapped mistake

18,000 feet

how these loose rocks got piled up here like this
when everything below builds up so steadily—
        a swoop a day long countries wide increases
        from deeper green into a paler leaning
        ice   then to this small pile and finally
        to room for each of us one at a time
        careful   of the cracking of the flag.
how piece by piece   stepped beyond   the element
of left and right   taken away, the sense of here
is made   all there is
under the feet,   all to come down
how much a freedom prison is
to what is   i
                                       learned.

romance

it is now known why the farmers
desert that fondling of their fields
why their wives give up the chickens
to the sly night that ferrets
the moon egg in the trough from between

the legs of the fence it is now
known why the children are hushed in
behind the lamps and the horses
excuse themselves into inconspicuous tufts
in the field's sleep because
it is embarrassing
this romance of empty space
that makes the open smell
of cowshit so untouchably near
that the white silo on the next farm
sweats with moonlight and accidentally
spills a slight stream of corn

suite

he went into   his room that no one there
and somehow open   closets   held his suits
his suits like him   held no one not even
the racks because like that the hold is nulled
the his of his suits' shoulders closed around
the fragile her
                    of metal fine except
she is his bone and he the style she wears.
he closed   the empty door no one behind him
since it was not her   and closed the closet.
what the
            police unhung yesterday
and folded must have been   was him only
in his shorts as if his suits were stolen.

the only night in town

the only night in town
operates one bar
in all the districts of its hours
this one establishment

the cheaper stars of glasses
set up shorter destinies
inside dream than dream's
dry open country

corked encompassed   seconds
line the bar up to the time
one breaks off the last note
of the loud high of a dime

in her ear   someone
clear enough the music
lets it reach the walls' gossip
of opposing mirrors

that the dead spot partnerless
on the floor goes as far
on as it comes   from
the only night in town

if the black frog will not ring

1

if the black frog will not ring
        it's the telephone)
i promise   my fingers
for its wart garden afruit with noise
and so much touch the civilization
cannot get its thumbs into its ears.

and it is wrong to go to bed and stay
and it is wrong to stay awake and play
                                        you didn't hear it so
again it is wrong
it is always wrong.

the frog's night
is the black night turned over   under covers
from the sun at both noons
the flashes before the eyes, squeezed tight,
are twenty moons   the tightness makes
the ears ring.

and it is wrong not to be home
and it is wrong to be someplace
                    else   an unreached party
or the wrong
address. me always as the wrong

2

exchange.   within the black frog's night
is the brand eyed dog
going from lance to lance to piss
upon the body

the skeletal trees   brittle reeds
the municipal legged insect
of streets   webs together

the will o' wisp of talk
pole to pole to somewhere
somewhere makes the black frog sing

queue (or the night traffic signals

it is for your own safety you must stand
back from the window. outside is about to go
off again. the edgy wall reflections and
the corner patterns are signals which i know
by now by heart by sheltered heart. the snappish red
and green   light in the fallow ceiling's plastic bath
(that is the dollar ten cent chandelier so deadened
with the algae of the night) like birds of wrath.

it is not considered that you know the world.
you must stand in the silver garden globe
where you'll be told. the main side of the room will break.
make no outcry. at times this launch of ends has hurled
a still green seeing eye through here. if it probes
its own distortion in your crystal   make it wait.

job

The pill to stay up dropped him through its arms.
and he has spent its time in its lost bed.
and it   down on its hands and knees in nightmare
on his chest   could still not find his eyes.
and this means that   this morning when it dies
before the hour squad of the sun run out,
the project   still   undone is its white carcass
on the desk without a line of life.

The sun has fired and his bright job is dead.
and sweating in his undressed suit he lies
where he fell   shirted and tied excuse.
blank morning finally blackens his name
to night Time itself pills with time yet on

His hands and knees he finds his corpse to draw on.

report

the subject was reported seen
facing a window at what seemed
to be a late reflection.

proprietors deny the window
or that anything at all
is in it anyhow.

a witness has been found who cost
his findings which were lost
among his life

but whose holdings are not official.
victims are advised
to pass or be satisfied.

BOATS, POEMS, FISH

IAN HAMILTON FINLAY

Sundial. Marbl

Sundial. Marble.

Many of the larger works are sited at the poet's home, Stonypath, Dunsyre, Lanarkshire, Scotland. They were made between 1967 and 1969. The photographer was Ronald Gunn. *Sundial, The Boat's Blueprint, Pond Inscription, Stem and Stern, Fisherman's Cross, KY* and *One Orange Arm. . .* were made in association with Maxwell Allan. *Sea-poppy 1* was made in association with Alistair Cant.

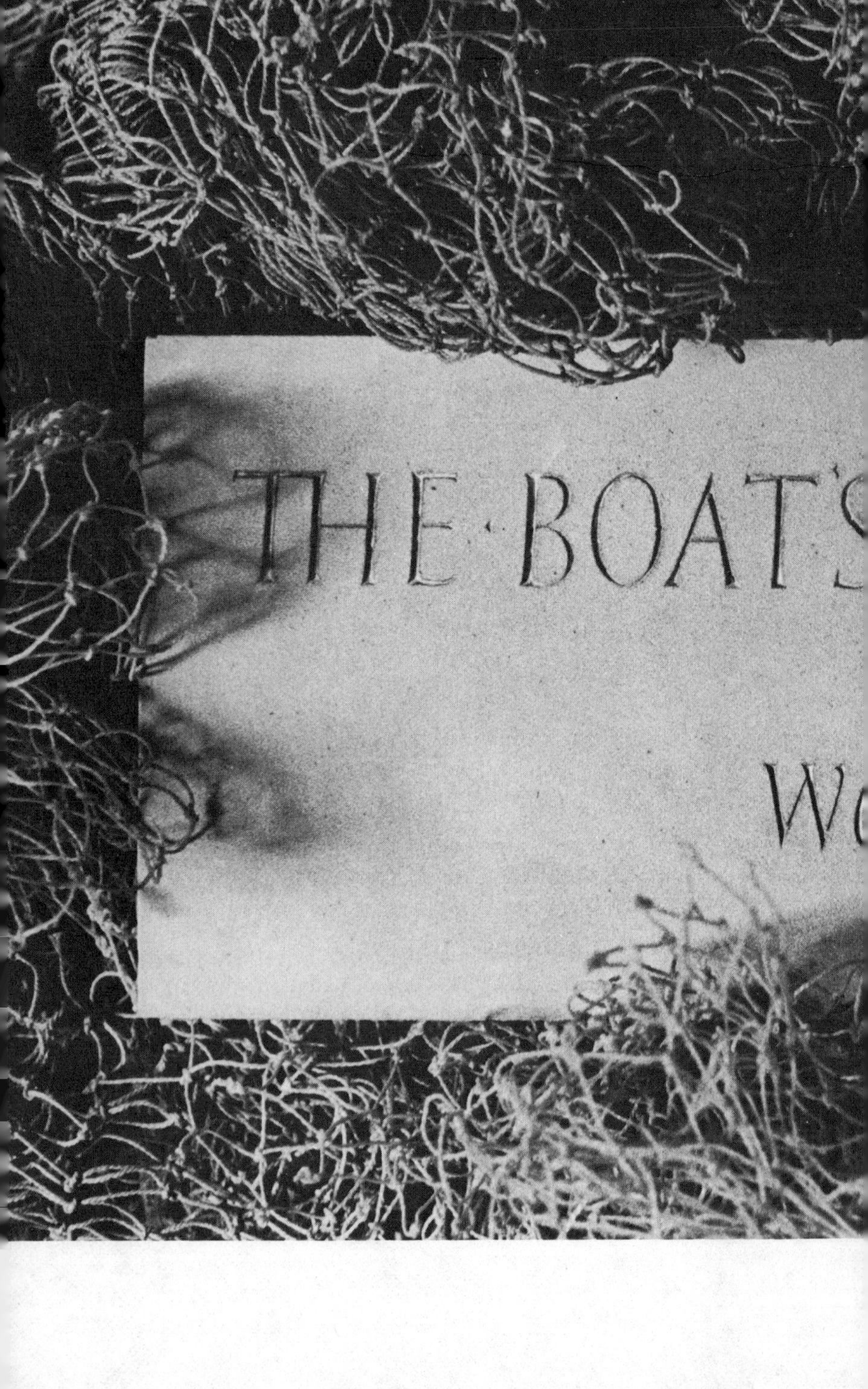
THE·BOAT'S

The Boat's Blueprint. Stone.

HIC·IACET
PARVULUM
QUODDAM
EX·AQUA
LONGIORE
EXCERPTUM

Pond Inscription. Stone.

Weathercock. Teak.

Stem and Stern. Stone.

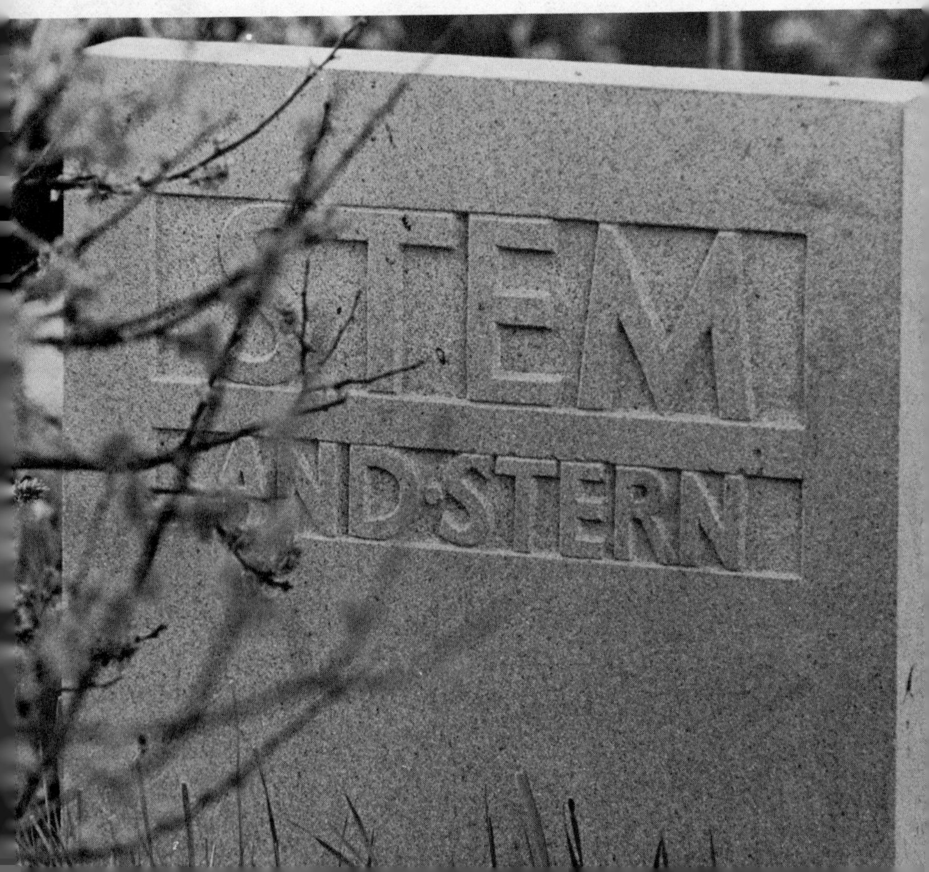

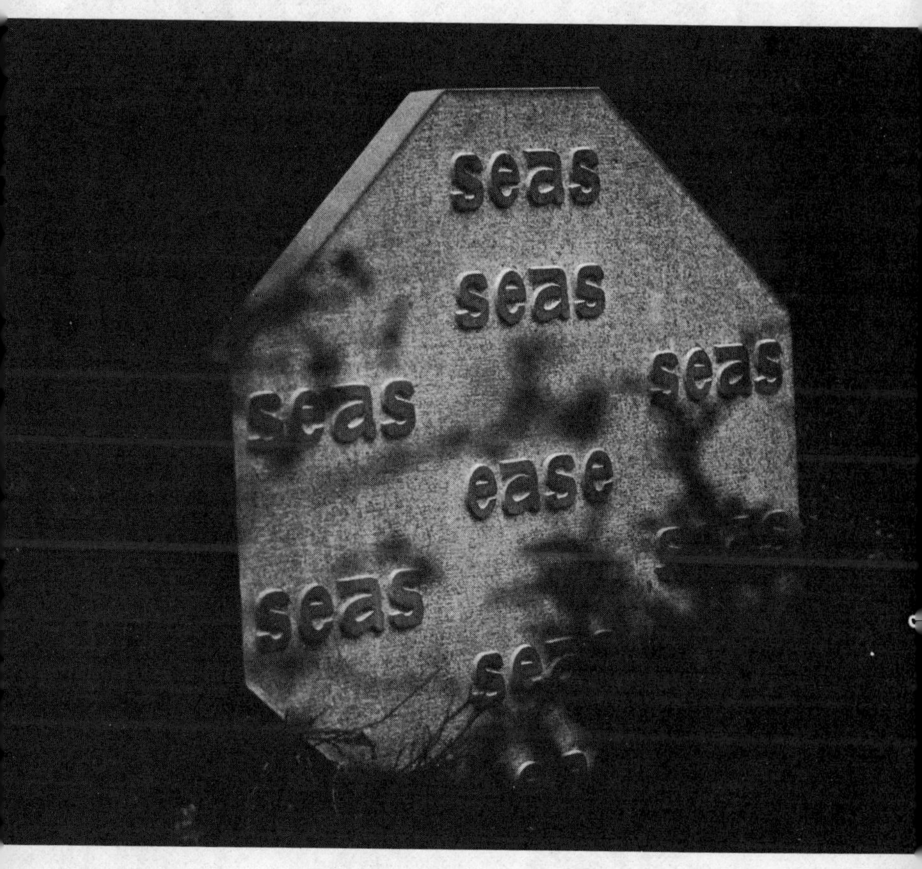

Fisherman's Cross. Blue slate.

Signpost. Painted wood.

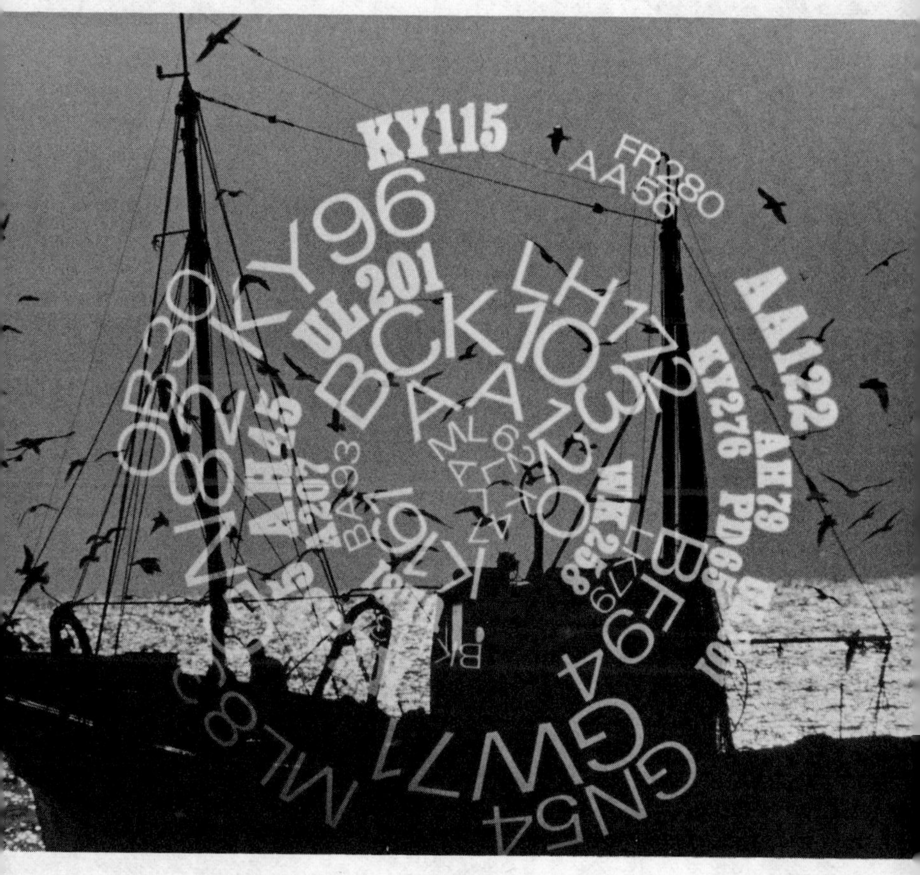

ea-poppy 1. Sandblasted glass. (Scottish fishingboat
ort-registration letters and numbers.)

KY. Cast concrete. (Design based on Kirkcaldy fishingboat port-registration letters.)

Water Weathercock. Painted wood.

Model Boats. (Model ketch and Scottish Zulu fishing lugger. Approximate length eight inches.)

The Land's Shadows. Sandblasted glass.

One Orange Arm. . . Stone.

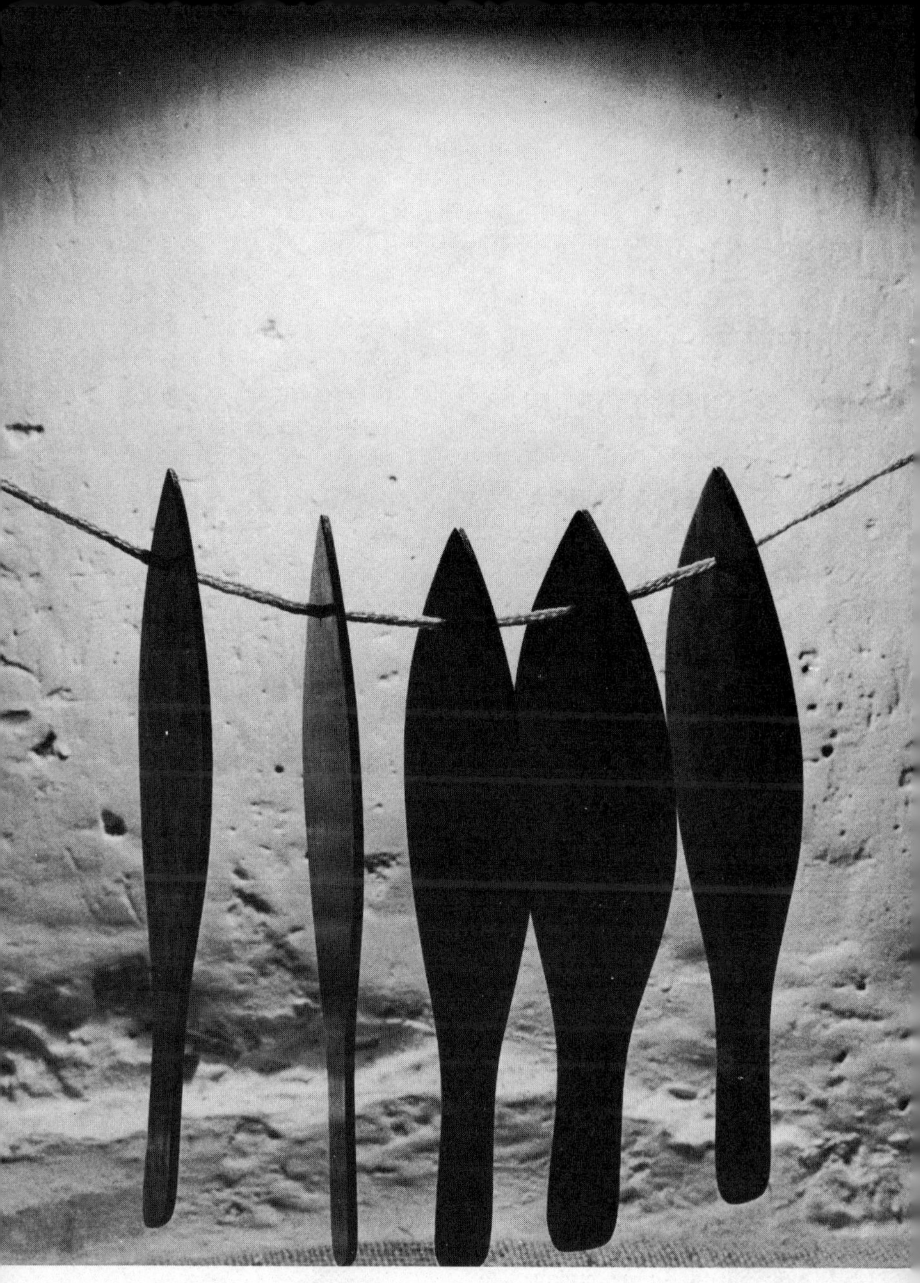

Wooden Fish. Painted wood.

EIGHT POEMS

RICHARD MEYERS

CELLS

Cells; their circuit, stamped
   A child in a cell and stamped the chemical scales,
Mechanical tracks, chemanical gears to ear
And tongue, and in the skull was
Fixed a friction.

So, first was forged
   A nightlong day, kept with a friend and a rough
Red knee. Then whammed to the core by
A new girl knowing grew the kid
To a boy and the

Boy became: frame
   Of the skull-wrapped rasp that age enlarged to
Shave decision tick by tick, and the grasp
Of the gears in the skin scared
The girl, scared up

These words, these words crying to
Split the source crying
These words.

POEM IN THREE PARTS

I stretched in the body, a condition of water;
Strict as an antler I (taught
In its learning) leaned.

Grown like a stick,
I spun hard in a spawning. Lied
In a sickness, the sickness spinning; a first birth
Lasted, I licked the kiss that
Stamped bones shut.

First past, I stretch in a body the quarrelled
Second. A second splitting till
:Snaps the spine.

THIS SIMPLE SEASON

This simple season, day, this weather
      Spills its weather, spilling
   Sun, left dripping lit
         Another Spring,
   And lights another.

That weather was which wet the brown grass
      Green, then stamped(as fast)
   Down hard(as dust)a
         Platform flat
   For animals, one
   Of which was me.

Or, we were two, as funny as knees, the
      Springs at once, we out-barked
   The splash of dogs—
         Responsibility in
   Clouds, the large
   Day, its ringing, the
   Springs at

Once. This sun, sun left dripping, now
    This season, season leans
  Me, reels loosely the
      Mornings, slings
  Back: a profusion
  Of dusks, packed
  In green, a slack of
  Springs, at once.

THE SHY SWARM IN HER THIGHS' WANING

The shy swarm in her thighs' waning: there
        Stops breath, fact
        Becomes. And her
Skin, bone-stretched between hips,

Its entrance, makes the throat's breath bone-
        Stretched also (the
        Breath—born deep like
Laughing and death-sprung, in the

Rush not for making but to make the rush last),
        Lashes guile, all words'
        Cunning, then *stops*,
Stops also and becomes sheer source.

DEATH'S NOVICE

Death's novice, I roar alive to
Death *Make me*
            spectacular, and
            reduce me
  Primitive as

Mineral. I am so airily furious—
Compact me
to density. So
said, though
Certain of

The sternness that restricts his motion
To the air
in which I'm
furious, and
Dying.

QUICKLY DARKNESS, YOU

Quickly darkness, you, resume me! Quickly re-
Plenish me. You equally despise the stupid
Rose and sky. Equal us of
Mindnessless and love.

Make me hard of objects, wide! with
Cracks. And stiff, quick with wide
Conditions, black and full
With darkness.

Black is the principle of our delight, is the
Principle of our belightful lack! We
Say *and,* and and!, and and
And *not!* We do.

IN THE MORNING

In the morning it is *angels* stretching; in the tall
Morning, in blue light

Every naked body's blood and barest hair
Is the hair and blood

Of an angel. So that the sun's sky: its air starts
At their breath, its
Warmth at their nerve, light unlocks from
Sockets of their eyes;

And in the lucid morning, in absolute quiet all the
Blue-lit angels *laugh,*
Roar! with the nothing that could be more fun
Than a world of angels.

And each naked body, with the same laughter, shakes
(To its blood, its hair)
To (its breath. its nerve. its eyes) its
Brain, where it wakes.

SET FORTH IN MYSELF

Set forth in myself for the skin of
The universe, galaxy to phallus I
Travel my infinite vein. I'm set
Forth in the sky for the skin of
Myself. So, is that the sun or
A cell in my skull? What atom
In this body makes me move?
If I find where I stop I'll know
The universe. I stop. The universe.

HONEY BEE

PAUL BRESLOW

We have the tenacity, the patience, the sheer ability to continue, the absolute thoughtless dedication to continuation of the fungus, but of course our group is still small, a handicap, but there is no chance whatever of our stopping because . . . because we know what we are doing. The fungus does not know; its growth ends and still it does not know. We know, and eventually we'll explain. A little shrillness, a certain countertenor tone, pure but weak, sounds in our resolution. I admit that. Why deny it? We can only grow, or die. No unplanted fields around us, nothing fallow in our climax community, yet we refuse to accept boundaries. We are severe and constant.

For two years I waited, nourishing myself, counting my talents, alone in my room on the twenty-first floor, never drunk, smoking cheap cigars pasted together with a glue that stinks when it burns, like overheated hide glue in the pot of a bootmaker. About me, on the walls, stuck to the ceiling, are pictures of lions, cats, tigers, lynxes—and bears. I can't resist them, the warm and clawing, the still-mammalian. Perhaps only Dorothy retains that same quality, of breathing and breeding and jumping over obstacles: the bestial potency. Of all of us, Dorothy, the first after me, is the least formed.

I would tear apart a pen, find in it the rubber sac—black, limp, and clogged with corroded dry carbon—sniff it, squeeze it, return it to its plastic capsule, and write. "A display of clay pipes such as are used in sewers. Natural concealment. Cold hard clay and experts and the bomb." That was at an early stage. The nidus of my cruelty: the invulnerability of others to my attack. I could conceive a victim, a means; but I lacked the courage. The dreading bravado of a cornered pigeon, the short stupid roll and fall of a dented hoop. The same pigeon might have sat on the shoulder of a poisoner with Cracker Jacks. The same hoop that I found in my mother's attic.

If only I could destroy myself. But I couldn't, for there would be no way to determine what my destruction might mean. I might, like Cafiero, cradle guilt for having secured more sun and rain than most; I might join the document, the explanatory note, the handbook of my death to my corpse, pinning it with *safety* pins to my skirt while still alive. It's impossible. They would merely infer a lie from the mode of my statement; they would cooperate with such part of my act as might be mad, but resist the rest. They would welcome madness, but withstand its reasons. Once, I thought I might make an Encyclopedia of Poetic Movements, restricted, bounded, and neatly defined. Not the movements you see in ballets, but the gestures of men and women freely made. Dying movements and living movements: no swans. Into whose hands, though, would such an Encyclopedia fall? An enemy's? Its trustee would hold my nature as the python holds a rabbit: prepared to merge it with muddy wastes, expelling bones and claws, teeth and nails, no resistance possible. I would be dead and the manuscript would be paper. I thought of carving names and signs, whole meaningful texts, tortuously minified, upon my teeth. Then something would remain to explain my bones. But not enough.

Specifics of assaults gathered at my feet. So grievous that I could no longer hope for self-defense, no less resistance, retaliation—or conquest. Not victory, conquest. I lived among the vicious and frightened, at one with hatred and cowardice. Every departure from my room became an emigration to a savage place, to the country of fear; of trial, defeat, insult, degradation, and pain. Men have not known fear; women have been raped. Men have been cowards; women have been raped. Men have run away; women have been raped. Set a ripe bud about to bloom in a cup of mercury: see it refuse to sink or float or slip away; it will consent only to burst. Imagine a garden of such events, pools of mercury and sinking vines.

Dorothy saved me.

Dorothy had a strange curved body, not deformed, but not remediable either, a natural look of being in a poor posture. Hair curled on her upper lip. I later shaved it off. Her lips were not repulsive, were in fact quite pretty, save for seeming a little stiff; but her body attracted, not her face.

Dorothy's body was very much like the body of the one I'd seen in the lobby of the Excelsior in Naples (in Naples, yes, not in Rome), the one who'd been watching a man in livery polishing the marble floor. The man did his polishing while standing up, by moving a rag back and forth with his foot (which was in a black shiny boot), the woman had been the one to whom I'd said, "Why do you think he does it standing up? Is it because he thinks this is more dignified? His standing up is a way of retaining his dignity?" She, the girl in Naples had replied, "Retaining isn't so difficult." But she had disappointed me.

Dorothy, in a cigar store in New York, wore a Marimekko dress with big white spots on a brown background; a patent-leather belt; brown plastic shoes with brass-plated buckles.

A gigantic man, with a beard looking like an old paintbrush stuck on his chin, but with no hair at all on his head, which was greasy, pushed her aside and thrust a dollar bill, very new and crisp, over the counter. He went out of turn, not only ahead of the girl, but also ahead of me, since I was next after her. He demanded a pack of Gauloises, but rejected a perfectly good pack of this very brand of cigarette and requested instead the Disque Bleu subvariety. He laughed deeply and knowingly and insultingly when the shopkeeper asked him if he meant the filter ones. He turned to me with a nasty smile on his face and said, using his lip muscles visibly, "Actually, they are not called 'the filter type,' they are called 'Disque Bleu.'" I can't speak French. I don't want to know how to speak French. English is foreign enough for me. I gave him not the slightest response, not the smallest ocular waver. He saw a hard, unsmiling woman in her forties, wearing a brown skirt, solid brown rayon blouse, and molded shoes. These shoes, though they are very expensive, look a bit like the ones worn by medieval peasants in old paintings.

I think I upset him. He left, after saying, "Give me."

The girl had dark brown hair, very straight and long.

I turned on my transistor radio, and it said, "We are waiting for your phone calls and the Lord is waiting too."

The girl froze. Before this, she had exhibited many of the little gestures most living people make when they are waiting in line, or "standing still." Her thigh muscles had rippled; her breasts had moved due to her breathing; she had touched her hair. Now for an instant she was truly still. Then she looked at me.

The shopkeeper also looked at me. But he first looked away; and, instead of freezing, he became more animated. His lips quivered; his nostrils flared. He reached down behind the counter, as if grabbing for a club or gun, but he stopped his motion short, pointed to me, and said, "Before this, I was on Madison Avenue. . . ." He seemed to be too upset to go on. I turned up the volume of the radio (an imprudent act, wasteful of the juices within the batteries).

"Pastor," said a woman's voice, "I have a spiritual problem. I receive no respect from my daughter, in spite of the fact that I've been saved." The pastor asked her when she had been saved, and she gave the date. "You have lost your fellowship with the Lord Jesus Christ," he said. "You're saved, once you're saved, well that's it lady, you've had it and you've been saved. But you can lose your fellowship." She had a pretty good fellowship, she insisted, this lady on the radio, but the pastor argued that she was in error. "Can you really believe that if you had your fellowship with Jesus Christ you would have a daughter who ran away from home and lived in sin and who has not been saved?" The woman was in doubt. "I don't know if she's that bad, my daughter . . . . I think maybe she just doesn't like me."

"Mother," said the girl in the cigar store. I turned off the radio.

"You want Kools, you don't want Kools, or you want French cigarettes?" the shopkeeper demanded. "I carry Disque Bleu," he added.

"Oh . . ." she said.

"My legs are swelling up from standing here," the shopkeeper said. "I have cardiac trouble and nocturnal headaches and last week my wife damaged her cornea."

"I don't know . . . ."

"You think I'm standing here for my health? I'm trying to explain to you: I've got cardiac trouble and my legs are swelling up . . . ."

"Kools."

"Here. Pay. Cash. *Next.*"

She experienced great difficulty in extracting her money from the leather pouch which she carried on a strap over her shoulder. This was because she had two paper bags in her arms and there was not room on the counter for her to set down the bags while dealing with the pouch. There were stacks of books by Henry Miller on the counter and a display of clear adhesive tape in various sizes. She was cheated on the change, but didn't notice. I followed her from the shop, not waiting to buy anything. I walked alongside her. She became uneasy. At the corner, waiting for the light to change, I addressed her.

"Was that really your mother?"

"Yes. Maybe. It sounded like her. She listens to the radio a lot, and she's been saved. But there must be others like her. Stupid people are always making those phone calls . . . ."

"Why don't you go home?"

"I do, sometimes. I don't think I will any more." She smiled, but she wasn't happy; I thought she was a hard girl. "My mother weighs eighty pounds. She doesn't say much, except over the radio—I mean, over the telephone—and the blinds are always drawn. She wears ribbons around her neck. Are you following me?"

"Yes."

"Please don't."

"Why not?"

"I don't know." Her answer apparently astonished her. "Because I don't know your name," she said. She dropped one of her paper bags. "It may not have been my mother." I picked up the bag, kissed it, and handed it to her. "I've never . . . ."

"It's all right," I assured her, at once fearing that I might lose her. "I'll go away." The light had changed to green, then back to red; there was no amber. "No I won't. I'm not going to let you get away."

She stepped off the curb, then crossed the street against the instruction of the light. She looked back once, walked on, became invisible. I plugged a tiny earphone into my radio, stuffed its vibrating nipple into my left ear, leaned against a lamppost, and waited. For an hour I waited, plugged in by a short cord to a small black box. I'm usually right when I wait.

She laughed at me for cleaning the earpiece with Kleenex; she took my arm and answered my questions in a low, polite voice. I brought her to my room.

At first I thought only of pleasure. My pleasure. To advance which end, I pushed her into a corner of the room, pinned her hands behind her, and, in the sweetest terms I could remember, painted for her in the brightest colors a picture of the most extraordinary glories I could recall or invent. In answer, she freed herself from my grip, fell upon her knees, and rubbed her face against my legs, extolling me in whimpers, as if, like a little dog, she had been beguiled by my tone of voice and my smell and had put herself at my use out of some low instinct for submission. I can't claim higher motives. I helped her, I think, to act her part more gracefully than she might have done without wise instruction; and I must take the major responsibility for leading her into what I must call a conspiracy, despite the fact that I had not in advance formed a definite intention. There had been others, but they hadn't seemed quite right.

She started to talk later, quite soon afterward, without much rest. "You are—you were—in love?" She asked this carelessly, as if unconcerned. I handed her a leather-covered diary. "With a man?" she wondered.

"No. Never. With neither man nor woman."

"But they must have, one of them, some of them loved you? You're not exactly ugly, you know, not even in that getup."

This was a bit inexact since, at the time, I had no clothing on. But I knew what she meant. I was pleased. Naturally her flattery pleased me, as did her interest in my emotions. "I doubt it very much," I said. It was good of her to assume that I might have emotions.

"You doubt that you're not ugly?"

"I don't doubt that, but I doubt that any of them were in love. Sometimes one would say he liked the way I did my hair. I wrote about some of them in the manuscript." She probably wouldn't understand what was in the manuscript. "I haven't let anyone read it, I didn't think . . . my penmanship isn't good either."

"I can type," she said.

Throughout our discussion she avoided the word "prostitute." My clients were considerate that way, too. Perhaps, like them, she regarded it as being an insulting word; she said that she listed herself as a secretary when she had to list such things. I had usually put down "Nothing" as my occupation; once or twice, I wrote "Whore." I was never refused credit, nor did anyone ever question me about that word; but they didn't like the "Nothing," which struck them as a bad joke. She asked me when I had stopped. Just "stopped."

"Two years ago," I said, "except for one or two occasions."

"When did you start wearing those shoes?"

"Also two years. The same time." They really are comfortable; but I'm not certain that I wear them for their comfort.

"The cigars too?"

"Everything changed . . . a short career, and careful investments. I suppose I'm rich."

She frowned. "You're—how old? About forty?" We were on my bed.

"Oh dear," I said, attempting to titter.

"Forty-five?"

"I'm thirty-seven."

I sometimes doubt the wisdom of honesty; especially when other people believe me. I've never raised an eyebrow over anyone else's dishonesty; yet most of the time I tell the truth.

She said she was twenty. Her neck was uncreased.

She leaned over me. "You should say 'my dear.' Leering and with that cigar, tapping the ashes—don't you care about the sheets?—you say 'I'm rich, my dear,' and then—I don't know—you should take a necklace or something from a wall safe. Twirl a dial and put your hand in the safe . . . ." She looked away, apparently thinking. "How much did you charge?" she asked.

"Anything I could get."

"Really? That's me. What was the highest?"

"Five hundred."

"I've gotten six and a trip to Miami." She smirked.

"But for how many days?"

She stopped smirking. "He ordered champagne with every meal," she said.

"That's very impressive."

She began to cry. I wiped her tears with her own hair, then dug my index finger deep into her neck. "Why did you do that?" she cried.

"To show you the sort of pain you ought to cry about." I did it again. "The jugular vein," I said. Her reaction to pain made her seem very stupid. She fluttered her eyelids, turning her eyes up drastically and exposing the ugly white part of her eyeballs. "Read the manuscript," I suggested.

"Okay. Calm down." She changed position and picked up the diary from the edge of the bed. Settling down on her back, she suddenly twitched, as if I'd hurt her again. "My God," she said, "that's a tiger on your ceiling." I told her it was a lion. "That's what I meant, a lion. I thought it was a cat before." I became certain that she wouldn't understand my notes, and I drowsed into a shallow nightmare. Perhaps I was still a little resentful of not being paid for so much effort; two years isn't such a long time. One had once come at me with a hot soldering iron; too many had done nothing at all. She hadn't asked me what my lowest fee had been. A bad dinner at the Four Seasons and insurance against getting a bullet in the heart; which may not have been a small profit.

She woke me by patting my belly with the diary. She was laughing, I think, though not necessarily at me.

"You," she said, "*you* are an *anarchist*."

"If you're planning to blackmail me," I warned her, "you won't have any luck. I won't pay you a cent."

She sat back on her haunches, like Rita Hayworth, that antique pinup, looking insulted and inviting and stupid. She said it was awful of me to think of blackmail. People have to trust each other, she said. I said I didn't think so and that in fact they didn't.

"You're very smart," she said.

I replied that she was too easily seduced. "It's easy to see why you're a whore," I told her. But it wasn't easy at all; she seemed quite normal and ordinary. I claimed that I was extremely ignorant, but that I had the ability of understanding my own beliefs. I admitted that I couldn't solve abstract problems and that I had a terrible time remembering the sorts of words, or collections of words, that people called "ideas."

"You have a strong head," she said, "and a beautiful vocabulary." She was in love with me. She had decided that I was crazy.

"I'm headstrong," I said, "but I sure as hell don't have a beautiful vocabulary." I pulled her hair. "Beautiful vocabulary, my ass." I kissed her breast. "Why don't you get out of here? What are you waiting for?" I shoved her. "Send your blackmail threats by mail."

"Wouldn't that make it a Federal offense?"

"I don't know. Shove them under the door, then. Just don't bother me."

She went in a sulky state to the shower, but returned in a few minutes, still wet, the water dripping to the floor, where it left permanent marks on the wood. Bangkok teak. She looked at me, shaking her head.

"You are an idiot," I said.

She continued to drip.

"I'll help you," she said.

My towels were all in the laundry, so I dried her off with paper toweling, which I wrapped around her mummy-fashion from the roll. I put on my bra and panties (which I have made for me of coarse unfinished silk by a tailor whose customers are mainly male homosexuals), and led her to my vanity. To my dressing table. I combed her hair with my tortoise-shell comb. The type of tortoise, with a very clear light shell, from which the comb was made, is becoming extinct, because certain Indonesians eat their eggs. It might be a good idea to picket the Indonesian consulate some day, to protest this waste.

"You want to kill people," she said, smiling at me in the mirror. "Let me use my electric razor on your little moustache."

"It's a problem, I admit."

"Not really. I like it. But you'll look better without it."

"I can—do it myself."

"You'll cut yourself. You're nervous."

"I usually do it myself."

"But not always?"

"When it's done, I do it."

"You just sit there like a good little girl."

She did just that. I combed her and shaved her and dressed her. I told her we needed eleven more women.

"It would be nice," she said, "if we could be certain that—we'd leave something behind."

"No one will ever forget," I said.

"That's what I mean." But the things she knows are things, and she will be gone long before them. Nothing new can really be destroyed, for true destruction, death, is the killing of a past. I asked her merely to restrict her future, to encircle her neck in token of this restriction. She accepted; she made several poetic movements that would have been suitable for inclusion in my Encyclopedia, if I had ever made it. Divert the fashion away from recording; frighten their feeble imaginations. Around her neck a pretty ribbon of wire, a golden chain, unremovable, light but unforgettable. Somehow she knew what would happen. "It doesn't matter," she said, "there are so many diseases you can get without risking anything at all."

"No one with ugly hands or stubby feet," I said. The links in the chain need not be beautiful; but they must be attractive and strong; gilded picture wire would do.

"It's crazy," she said, shaking her head, feeling the slight weight of the thin necklace.

I saw that she had doubts; but I did not see a doubting woman. "Did even ten percent of them seem human to you?" I asked. "Can you pity them? Can you think of them as your children?"

"I follow you," she said. Pouting, she had another doubt. "What if—what if we make a mistake?"

"All of us? We'll discuss everything first, and there will be a rule of unanimity. We can't make mistakes."

I grasped her chin and pushed her head up. I stared at her nostrils: they were perfect, exactly symmetrical, whether divided naturally by the vertical axis of the septum, or artificially by an imagined horizontal axis.

"I'll take the responsibilty. If there are mistakes—I'll be the first to go," I said.

This satisfied her.

"Risk," she said softly.

I had begun to move out of the night; I had found her, she would help me to find the others, and in their company I would be able to leave my room without fear and without a sense of being false and vulnerable. One's eyes hurt when leaving the dark. I could not imagine myself killing people; but I could imagine it well as something mixed into the acts of others, as cooperation in revenge, as the protective gathering around a sigh. I was excited, of course; my senses proposed motions outside categories. I gained courage; lost nothing. I had been enlarged, not coarsened; there would be more of me and less of the world, and yet nothing dwindled in my sight. I could see more and further ahead; my head ached, but less with pain than with the shuddering receptivity that runs before both pain and pleasure—the purr before eating or sleeping, the same purr before pouncing or dying.

"I think I'm afraid of you," she said. It was the nicest thing she could have said. Doctors inject sugar solution to relieve varicose veins; it's a cowardly way to hide your age; and, if people didn't die, their weight would soon exceed the earth's. I never even wear makeup any more; but I've retained a supply.

I took my best jade snuffbox, opened it, caressed with the tip of one finger the buttery cosmetic it held, and lightly, with untrembling touch, covered the shadows beneath her eyes. I could feel her pores. I could feel her lashes flutter.

"Do you think we'll be caught?" she asked.

At that moment I approached the condition of the honey bee, which is so sensitive it can feel the movement of particles in its own blood.

THE WORLD WITHOUT WORDS

RYUICHI TAMURA

Translated by Samuel Grolmes and Yumiko Tsumura

1

The world without words is a mid day globe
I am vertical

The world without words is a world of the poetry of noon
I can not remain horizontal

2

I will discover the world without words using words
I will discover the mid day globe the poetry of noon
I am vertical
I can not remain horizontal

3

Mid day in June
The sun overhead
I was surrounded by rock

And
The rock was a corpse
the lava corpse
of the energy of
some volcano
Why was all form
just then the corpse of energy
Why were all colors and rhythms
just then the corpse of energy
One bird
for example a golden eagle
observed but did not criticize
in its smooth circling
Why did the golden eagle
just then do nothing but watch
the form of energy
Why didn't the golden eagle
just then try to criticize
all color and rhythm
The rock was a corpse
I drank milk
ate bread like a foot soldier

4

Oh
The flow of incandescence that rejects fluidity
The flow that love and fear cannot shape
The form of cooled flame
All forms of dead energy

5

A bird's eyes are exactly wickedness
He observes he does not criticize
A bird's tongue is exactly wickedness
He swallows he does not criticize

6

Look at the tongue of a nutcracker torn out sharply
Look at the tongue of a woodpecker the spear of some pagan god
Look at the tongue of a woodcock the sculptor's knife
Look at the tongue of a thrush the smooth murderous weapon

He observes he does not criticize
He swallows he does not criticize

7

I
walked down a road cold as the back of the moon
walked down the thirteen miles to the cottage
along the stream of lava
along the road of death and procreation
along the road of ebb-tide I have never seen
I am a foot soldier
or else
I am a shipwrecked sailor
or else
I am a bird's eyes
I am an owl's tongue

8

I watch with blind eyes
I fall down with my blind eyes open
I stick out my tongue and destroy the bark
I stick out my tongue but not to caress love and justice
The thorn harpoon on my tongue is not for curing fear and starvation

9

The road of death and procreation
is the road of small animals and insects
The swarm of honey bees which soars away raising a battle cry
one thousand needles in ambush   ten thousand needles
The road without criticism and anti-criticism
of no meaning of meaning
of no criticism of criticism
The road that has no vain construction or petty hope
The road that has no need for metaphor for symbol or imagination
There is only destruction and procreation
There is only a fragment and a fragment inside a fragment
There is only a sliver and a sliver inside a sliver
There is only the pattern inside the enormous pattern on the ground
The road of a cool June simile
The air sac sent from a red lung
The air sac like an ice bag filling the air to the marrow
The bird flies
The bird flies in a bird

10

A bird's eyes are exactly wickedness
A bird's tongue is exactly wickedness
He destroys he does not construct
He re-creates he does not create
He is a fragment   a fragment inside a fragment
He has an air sac but does not have an empty heart
His eyes and tongue are exactly wickedness he is not wicked
Burn   bird
Burn bird   all birds
Burn   bird   small animal   all small animals
Burn   death and procreation
Burn   road of death and procreation
Burn

11

June cold as the back of the moon
Road cold as the back of the moon
On the road of death and procreation
I run down
I drift
I fly

I am a foot soldier
yet I am the brave enemy
I am a shipwrecked sailor
yet I am the ebb-tide
I am a bird
yet I am the blind hunter
I am the enemy
I am the brave enemy

12

Finally I
will reach the cottage in sunset
Thin little shrubs will change into huge forests
The lava stream and the sun and the ebb-tide
will be shut off by my little dream
I will drink a glass of bitter water
I will drink it quietly like poison
I will close my eyes and open them again
I will cut my whiskey with water

13

I will not return to the cottage
I can not dilute a word with meaning
as I do my whiskey with water

from

SUNDAY THEY'LL MAKE ME A SAINT

(Two Scenes of a Play)

DEMETRIUS K. TOTERAS

[*The scene is in a prison, where imaginary beings enter the playwright's cell and act out his fantasies. Earlier in the play, the characters have conducted the trial of Picalo, found him guilty, and are now preparing for his execution and canonization. The characters are all masked, except for the Reverend; Luther, Amile and Picalo all wear identical masks.*—Editor]

There are moments that I sit here and see the exact place where Mama Spider is standing, and Luther is sitting behind the trunk. The Harlequin is sitting on the edge. Cleopha is sitting on the bucket, Amile on the cot. The Reverend is standing next to Luther.

LUTHER. Tell us, Mama, why did you go up to the hill?
It's been years since you came last.

MAMA SPIDER. I love growing flowers and carrying them.

LUTHER. I have to ask you something and it seemed to me that it was a good way to begin.

REVEREND. She has no way of knowing why she does anything.

AMILE. For that reason it should be that we let her go and not bother with her any more.

LUTHER. For that reason we should keep her here and find out if she could pass that over to us and fill us up with her wisdom, if that is what you're telling me it is.

MAMA SPIDER. It's you who doesn't know! (*She stares at Luther.*)

LUTHER. Then I have the wisdom, Mama. Thank you. (*Luther yells.*) . . . Blue rider. . . (*Picalo backs up from the open hole that is in front of him.*) . . . The dirt is the rider for you and you shall feel its weight until it cleans your flesh off your hulking bones.

(*The Harlequin brings on the stage an olive crap pot, orange paint fallen down its sides, and leaves it next to Mama Spider.*)

MAMA SPIDER. What's this?

LUTHER. A pot! What do you think it is?

MAMA SPIDER. What for?

LUTHER. To fill your fears in it so that we may save them and pass them out to whoever needs them. . .

Even the shirt that I have on me now. . .
It's close pinstripes, blue on white or white on blue.
It should be hung next to a pair of silk pants,
my shirt upside down and pants right side up. . .
It should become my altar where I'm going to go and pray
and at night you shall hear me howl like a jackal.

MAMA SPIDER. I don't want to hear the noise. It irritates me.

CLEOPHA. Has Luther said something that you might not like hearing, Madam? If so, you might tell us this moment.

MAMA SPIDER. There is nothing that I want to say to any of you.

AMILE. Then why did you come?

MAMA SPIDER. To find where Picalo is going.

LUTHER. All you had to do was ask us and we would have told you, just as simple as that. . . But you had to tell us more than that didn't you? Standing there, offended, a theater that you built and used us as bricks. . . Do as you're told Picalo!

(*Picalo takes off his boots and places them on the trunk as he was told. The front of the shoes are turned up and they look as if they have started to turn his toes up with them.*)

CARNATION. The imagination has no sex. It has no form. It has no full character. . . A pair of shoes could be your father. It could have been your lover whom we're looking at. It could be whatever we want it to be, don't you think, Mama?

(*Mama Spider looks around at all the faces that have gathered around the shoes.*)

LUTHER. They are beautiful.

REVEREND. Amen.

LUTHER. Talk to the shoes, Mama. Talk to them and see what they tell you. You can ask them anything you want and they will give you some answer, at least an answer that will not be taken as that of Picalo but only as the shoes that Picalo wore.

SHOES. Well what do you want to know?

(*Mama Spider looks around the room and there is no one there anymore.*)

[She is by herself like a child who has been caught in
its dream naked. . .
The orange color of the pot lifting itself up filling the
air about her with fear,
the king who held the world from its tentacles sees it
slipping from his hands and screams. . .]

SHOES. Whatever it is you want to say, say it to me. Is it a lament that you have?

MAMA SPIDER. No, not a lament.

SHOES. Then it could be that you have been wronged by someone.

MAMA SPIDER. Yes! That's what it is. . . I have been wronged by the offspring that I had.

SHOES. You should not be afraid as I sit here in front of you to tell me exactly what it is that you feel.

MAMA SPIDER. I feel a horror that has possessed me. . . greater than I have ever felt before.

SHOES. This is exactly what I want you to tell us if you can.

MAMA SPIDER. I'll try. (*The Shoes start laughing.*) . . . What are you laughing at? My horror?

SHOES. No! At the fact that you're going to tell me and I'm going to listen.

MAMA SPIDER. But you asked me to tell you.

SHOES. It's better that we tell you. Then it would make no difference if we're right or wrong, only in the fact that we said something.

MAMA SPIDER. (*She turns and looks around.*) Where did everyone go?

SHOES. They found no reason to stay around here and listen to what we're going through, so they left.

MAMA SPIDER. I could have had everything I wanted once and I let it go so I wouldn't be blamed for misuse of my time.

SHOES. That's no excuse. You would have been blamed anyway.

MAMA SPIDER. You brought me here to trounce on me like a hen in a gravel pit!

SHOES. It is not the Man you came to see. It is not the flesh and the bones. . . It is the master whom one looks for. It is the stuff that reaches above the carcass and the willows. It is that aurora which fills the nostrils of an open bottle, the fume of time and the relegation of the essence which raises above the open hole and the bleakness of an eternity.

MAMA SPIDER. You should not have stopped, Shoes. You should have gone on.

SHOES. I could have but there was more. . . It was the leaves that fell, the petals of Carnation's words. The reflection from a copper amulet froze the corridors, froze the passages here on my soul.

MAMA SPIDER. Shoes, I came here to mourn and to lament Picalo and you have led me to lament for you.

SHOES. I want to answer you but not as a pair of shoes that have been taken from the feet of soldiers and placed on the feet of Saints.

(*Voices are heard from behind the stage.*)

VOICES. (*murmuring*) Why must we be forgotten?

SHOES. You must remain dead and anonymous.
You died unwilling. You died for no reason.
Stay dead and forgotten!

(*The Reverend walks back to the cell.*)

SHOES. (*looking at The Reverend*) What do you want?

REVEREND. It is my job to administer to the dead.

SHOES. Then you should join them, Reverend, and not let the curtain of time separate you from your loved ones, from your children and your flock.

(*The Reverend puts his hands on the paper chains that I have wrapped around him.*)

[I would have wanted, as I said, to have put steel ones

on him, iron wrought chains so he could feel what it was to have them stop him from scratching his ass, from wiping his nose.]

SHOES. I have really nothing against you, Reverend.

REVEREND. Thank you, Shoes.

SHOES. And you, Mama Spider, you should feel the same.

(*Carnation comes back into Picalo's chamber. The walls are adorned with lights turning from red, yellow, to blue. The highly polished floor is glimmering, dancing from chips of reflecting material strewn on it.*

SHOES. (*looking at The Reverend*) Though we could have been enemies, Reverend, I let the word roll from my tongue, friend. Both of us have looked at the world from the bottom of a charred bucket.

REVEREND. It is your integrity that I have thought of.

SHOES. And. . . Reverend?

REVEREND. And you have none.

SHOES. You can not be actor and God at the same time.

(*The Reverend takes his hands from the paper chains he is holding and with his right hand he scratches his ass.*)

CARNATION. You should take your choice, Shoes, now that you have the chance.

VOICE. What have I done, Shoes, that you have forgotten me so soon? (*The Voice moans from behind the stage.*)

SHOES. I chose not to judge you so I served you. I stayed with you.

MAMA SPIDER. (*She goes to the bucket and sits down.*) I am old and to stand bothers me. . . A red petal and a string of pearls, a golden hat so I can sit and weep.

(*The Reverend goes to Mama Spider and starts to touch her, then his hands stop and he falls to his knees.*)

VOICES. (*moaning*) What of us? Hold us in your hands and let the sweetness roll down the empty banks!

SHOES. Shut your mouths! You're disturbing the thoughts that go between me and Mama Spider.

VOICES. And what have you said that we should not be part of you? What have we done that you should have walked off from us?

SHOES. You died for nothing. . . I couldn't be hung on you and left to rot!

VOICES. All of us have been forgotten.

SHOES. Not all of you. . . Some are remembered when new ones fill your ranks, when they walk out of their barracks, raw, bleeding at the heart for a chance to show their loved ones that there is more in them than just a glimpse of hair on their face.

VOICES. They shall remain forgotten when they wear the white mask, their jaws broken where their hatred passed through.

(*The Guard comes walking in. He has a uniform that looks like an Army uniform.*)

GUARD. The Voices have been forbidden to complain. It is sacrilegious. It is against the world of the Man that they speak.

SHOES. I don't give a fuck. Make it your own affair. My obligation to them has ended when they took me off of them and laid them all together in that hole.

GUARD. You have a duty to protect the secret.

SHOES. The secret has been told. I say nothing new.

MAMA SPIDER. It would have been so wonderful had Amile died wearing you. Pride in his unseeing eyes, frozen there till the maggots ate the pride and took it with them to become the proud maggots of the hole.

GUARD. They were laid out with their medals and a bugle blew and a line of friends stood over them, lifted their legs and fired a last farewell.

SHOES. The cheap brass was used to fill the gaping holes that were drilled in them.

VOICES. (*yelling*) Bastards, you toy with our memory!

SHOES. Don't scream at me! I walked along with you. I felt the frozen North till I became as hard as stone.

Guard. You are indeed a well-walked pair of shoes.

MAMA SPIDER. What could I have done? His prick created all my problems.

SHOES. If it had not been his, then it would have been someone else's that you let crawl in you, spitting at you, forming the universe that would soon consume us.

MAMA SPIDER. (*She sounds exhausted.*) Amile, Luther, Picalo? All three?

GUARD. (*looking at her*) You better not let the Man hear it. He has sworn to erase all resistance, to make all of you function in eloquence. You will be given your thoughts and you will refine them, then you will see that the Man will be happy again.

VOICES. We've been cheated again. He told us the same thing.

(*Six soldiers come in wearing Army uniforms. They stand like store dummies around the Shoes.*)

GUARD. You see? The Man had heard already.

SHOES. You see the marks on my side? All of you, do you see them?

They're piss marks. . .
the last thing that came from the last one who wore me.
Long after his jaw fell open, he peed.

(*The soldiers lift up sticks and hold them over the Shoes.*)

His final testimonial to the gallant life. . .

(*One of the soldiers hits the Shoes.*)

His final offering to the God of the earth. . .

(*And another soldier hits him with the stick.*)

He gave all he had, even his last piss. . .

(*They hit again. The Shoes' voice becomes weak.*)

The marks on my side show, it was his medal, his speech, his last will. . .

(*Another soldier hits them.*)

It shall be your last doing. . .

(*All the soldiers start hitting the Shoes. The Guard watches. Mama Spider puts her hands over her face.*)

GUARD. Look at it, Mama Spider. The Man is not happy to do this.

VOICES. There'll be others, you bastards! There'll be others who'll come and they'll yell it out loud, louder than you can fart over.

(*The lights start flashing yellow, blue, and red. Luther comes running in.*)

LUTHER. You bastards! Get out!

(*Amile is lying on the bed. The Reverend is kneeling. Luther stands over Amile.*)

LUTHER. Why did you let them come? Why did you let them come now? I'm tired of this farce and the Voices and the Shoes. . . Get on your feet, Reverend! Get on them feet of yours. Let them know that I have made my choice and it is not for blurping idiots to try to avenge my decision. . . We'll bury Picalo along with his shoes so those who come after us will know that we lived. (*He laughs loudly, then stands up and screams.*) Big Fella, you brute, you motherless whore!

(*Big Fella comes into the cell empty-handed.*)

LUTHER. Where's the rope?

(*Big Fella looks at Luther, then his eyes look at everyone there.*)

> [I can't remember how he sounded when he told us that the Man took his pet.]

BIG FELLA. The Man took it from me.

LUTHER. Then make one out of palm leaves or your pants, your shoestrings. That's what Fatty used when he told the world he was going to start over again, some other time, some other place.

CARNATION. (*looking at Big Fella*) Oh, he's like a huge bull. Shoestrings wouldn't hold him up with his neck nestled between the prickly thyme tearing at the white silk, eating ferns laid on the marble steps that lead to the waiting darkness, the velvet ooze of emptiness. . . (*Carnation walks toward Big Fella and commands him to get on his knees.*) On your knees, Big Fella! No. . . better yet, get on all fours. I'm going to pet you.

(*A drummer walks into the cell. He has on a pointed crimson hat.*)

CLEOPHA. You could have dressed him at least.

LUTHER. A hat is all he needs and that drum, the rest he can do without.

(*The drummer is rolling the sticks on the drum.*)

LUTHER. Stand up all of you! The burial of Picalo is going to take place. (*He walks to the edge of the stage and looks at the audience. His voice is loud but not angered.*) Stand up all of you! We've entertained you long enough. Stand up and help us bury Picalo. (*He runs back to the other actors who are waiting for him.*)

AMILE. No one is going to say anything about this. Do you hear? If anyone finds out we've had it. . . All of you raise your hands, both hands, maybe that would be better. And repeat after me: In the name of all those who have gone before us we swear to break out of this hole.

(*All the actors repeat the lines after him.*)

AMILE. We will keep the whereabouts of the hollow baby that was once Picalo, a secret.

(*The actors repeat after him.*)

AMILE. David danced around the Ark and we around the hollow baby.

REVEREND. What the Hell do we do with him?

ALBINO. Stuff him down the toilet. Let the fish have him.

CLEOPHA. Fat fish. . . Oh what a thought!

LUTHER. He wanted it that way.

CLEOPHA. Poor Picalo!

LUTHER. Saint Picalo! I'll swear I saw him lift up over the walls on a Sunday morning and take off with a band of angels.

REVEREND. Oh what a thought to live with!

AMILE. That's good enough. Did all of you see it? (*He hears a grunt from the actors.*) Well?

ACTORS. Sure we did!

(*Big Fella brings in Picalo's body and lays it on the trunk. Picalo is stiff, like an iron bar, the shoes are on him, the toes are not curled.*)

CARNATION. Doesn't he look smart?

REVEREND. This place will be reeking in a few days and someone might question Picalo's abilities.

MAMA SPIDER. What of my feelings? I should be seen crying, something draped over me at least, Cleopha and Carnation holding me, Pink Lizard carrying my change of clothes.

CLEOPHA. I wonder what he thought in the last minute.

REVEREND. Hovis and Big Fella took care of it.

LUTHER. (*looking at Harlequin*) Send out an order, tell them all, to all the prisons, paste it up on every railroad yard, on the inside of every boxcar leaving an outbound yard. . . Picalo has been done in by the Man. (*Luther walks up to where Picalo is laid out and the actors follow him.*) You shall be remembered, Picalo, as long as there's beauty in life.

AMILE. Let's put a tent over him and we can all go and say our last farewell.

LUTHER. Who will go first?

REVEREND. It should be you, Luther. You've earned the right.

LUTHER. Maybe you're right. . .

(*Luther goes into the tent. Loud farting and laughing are heard coming from it.*)

MAMA SPIDER. (*walking around the tent*) Can I look in?

LUTHER. (*yelling from inside the tent*) I'm not through yet! To get him ready you really have to work him over good.

(*Cleopha is standing next to Carnation, holding her rags and looking at the ground.*)

CARNATION. (*She turns to look at Cleopha but speaks as if to herself.*) I could have been a rose or a lily.

AMILE. Or the splotches of dried piss on my pants.

CLEOPHA. It's Spring. . . It's Spring and all of it will come back again.

LUTHER. (*He comes from the tent, wiping his hands on his pants.*) All through! and what a piece of art it is! (*He looks at Amile.*)

AMILE. You're a born bastard, Luther.

LUTHER. I'm born. That's the only thing that's important. . . How I came makes no difference to me, only to Mama Spider. Isn't that right, Mama? (*He turns to her as she stands next to the tent, still looking at it.*)

(*From behind the actors the Voices again raise their anguish.*)

VOICES. And we shall be forgotten we know. . . (*The whole tier is banging on the bars.*) We shall be forgotten!

LUTHER. All I can remember is how cold my feet were and Picalo telling me to kill the Chinaman to take his clothes . . . Amile, let's bow our heads then for the Chinaman. (*Luther turns and looks at the Reverend.*)

REVEREND. Yes Luther?

LUTHER. Reverend, read to us from your memory.

REVEREND. I remember very little and because I don't have to remember, I walk up and down the hill. . . its grass eaten short by hungry flocks looking for the days I spent watching them.

AMILE. Soldiers shoot, they don't kill. Men kill and they are hung.

(*Cleopha walks over to the tent and prepares to go inside. She hesitates and Luther watches her.*)

LUTHER. (*yelling*) Holy Shit! He's almost a Saint and you sit on the threshold of the Saintdom and fiddle around with your doubts.

REVEREND. Christ! I've never been to a Saint's baptism. Saint

Picalo. . . what a name! No wonder the poor bastard never knew about it. It could have been Saint Flute stuffed up to his armpit fondling the empty holes with his fingers. . . Christ man, that's all Picalo had left on him, the tips of his fingers and his toes, the rest of him had been consumed by that Pink Lizard. . . (*He walks around pounding his head as if it had just cleared. Luther lies on the ground and starts laughing.*) This is no joke. We created a legend, Man, with our crap. We created a myth that will go on long after this fart-bag disappears. Even Mama Spider is going to get it. (*He looks at her on her knees, she is crying.*) Why you shallow string of piss, you're damn near famous and you can't see the piss rolling down my legs! I can't take it standing. . . (*He leaps on the floor with Luther, both heaped on each other, laughing.*)

(*The Harlequin comes in. He raises a horn to his lips and blows it. A shrill sound comes from it. Big Fella comes in and behind him the Guard who has a horn that makes the sound of a siren.*)

LUTHER. We have no time to lose at all. Big Fella grab the hollow baby. . .

(*Mama Spider reaches down for the bucket filled with water and washes her hands.*)

LUTHER. You can't clean them, Mama Spider, not with that water.

(*Cleopha looks at the body of Picalo; her head is now bent low. The rag doll she has drops from her hands. The lights keep turning and the doll becomes lost in color. Big Fella grabs Picalo's body. Pink Lizard comes walking in beating a drum.*)

LUTHER. There's no time for a big thing of this. The whole place is in a turmoil. Get rid of him and we'll figure it out later.

HARLEQUIN. Where do we put him?

LUTHER. Make sure no one finds him, that's all. The rest we'll leave to the Reverend to take care of . . . (*Luther looks at the Reverend.*) You know how, Reverend.

REVEREND. I know how it's been done. I think I can do it.

LUTHER. Good. Then let's get going.

HARLEQUIN. Should we make another scene for it?

LUTHER. Why bother? The event is greater than the reason.

(*Picalo stares at Me as they pull him out. The siren and horns stop. The Voices in the tiers are mumbling. Amile's been shot going over the wall.*)

a note on
SUNDAY THEY'LL MAKE ME A SAINT

JAMES POTTS

Demetrius Toteras is a Greek. He is also an American. He was sentenced to thirty years in prison. He wrote *Sunday They'll Make Me a Saint* while serving his sentence. It is a major work of dramatic art, not as some might claim, the document of a paranoiac schizophrenic. Some will see his work within the tradition of the Absurd, others as an archetypical Happening, but I think to try to label this work for the sake of academic discourse, would relegate the author to a circumscribed area and forbid the work its natural propensities in speaking for itself.

To place Toteras in a historical perspective is futile. He ranges from the humor of Aristophanes to the buffoonery of the Commedia dell' Arte, from the dark psychological drama of Strindberg to the ruthless and wild invocations of Antonin Artaud, from the ritualistic murders of the Marquis de Sade to the indifference of its modern counterpart; all of it combined in a whirling mind which finds no rest, no explanations, no answers, an internal world governed by its own laws.

Antonin Artaud's explanation of drama and his reference to the metaphysical man is as close as one can exemplify Toteras and *Sunday They'll Make Me a Saint:*

"The theatre will never find itself again—i.e. constitute a means of true illusion—except by furnishing the spectator with the truthful precipitates of dreams, in which his taste for crime, his erotic obsessions, his savagery, his chimeras, his utopian sense of life and matter, even his cannibalism, pour out, on a level not counterfeit and illusory, but interior. In other terms, the theatre must pursue by all its means a reassertion . . . of the internal world, that is, of man considered metaphysically. It is only thus, we believe, that we shall be able to speak again in the theatre about the rights of the imagination." One might feel that in using Artaud's explanation we could begin to understand *Sunday They'll Make Me a Saint,* but the inner world of fleeting fantasies, dreams and hallucinations are not reached and understood as easily as the realities of the objective world. One can be approached through measurement, comparison, logic, philosophical systems and the expendiency of "isms." Though useful for what it was intended, it lacks qualitative meaning and becomes a useless appendage in the attempt to investigate the metaphysical man whose existence is an unfamiliar world, a universe undescribable by the senses.

The historical division between the exterior and the interior existence of man has never been more evident in the dramatic arts and art in general, than in the last two decades. A tired society, tired of systems that have brought about two great wars, of explanations concerning normality; a philosophical system that has failed to provide no more than technological refinements, has given vent to a generation of dramatists who feel that to be shackled to the convention which ignites one for the purpose of general understanding is the overture of death. "After us, the Savage God," prophesied W. B. Yeats, when he and his friends witnessed the first performance of Jarry's *Ubu Roi. Sunday They'll Make Me a Saint* is the first true manifestation of the savage god. The monster's hour has come around to devour us. It's the renouncement of discourse concerning "being," no swaddling clothes to strip off to get to the core, to the essence of the savage god. It "is" without any attempt of apology by Toteras.

"Being" and the description of "being" are the primary difference between art and the philosophical. One "is," the other attempts to "be." There is no hero in the play to attribute dramatic climaxes. There is no horizontal line of reasoning to lead the viewer through the labyrinths of Toteras's mind. The structure of the play is a compressed morphological stratification where all superlatives have been expelled, each strata independent from the other, containing its own fantasies, its own ruthlessness and cunning, its own savagery and desire for life, hallucinations that recreate their own mirages, imagos that have their own phantoms. The play is more like a work of sculpture where one sees it from various positions, viewing it always for the first time, revolving continuously in front of one's eyes. It is more like electronic music than the classical symmetry of contrivance. No effort is made by Toteras to explain the unexplainable. Camus, in the *Myth of Sisyphus,* explores the attitude: "A world that can be explained by reason, however faulty, is a familiar world." Things just happen in the world of Toteras. The "why" they happen has no validity. "The event is greater than the reason," one of his characters states.

In order for Toteras to analyze his position, he would be forced to argue the absurdity of his environment. The prison, where the work was written, is merely a backdrop, the cell, a stage. The confinement and the nightmare existence of the prisoners are not used as an exploitation for material or for didatic plot structure: it is merely an ever present light bulb shining in his eyes. It is a colorless wall that he fills with his paintings or the strange prison sounds of whistles and horns; his only lament: "All the thoughts that I brought with me in this bleakness I found to have been of no use, again from the beginning to relearn that which can't be understood."

Like Blake, Toteras paints each mental scene on canvas. The play is filled with a kaleidoscope of color and the visual imagery of the paintings are retranslated into a dramatic form. The interior of the play becomes a mirage where one is led to believe that Amile is Toteras, only to find that Amile is dead. We assume Luther is Toteras, or possibly he has been created by Toteras as a psychological necessity, a depository for his emotions, only to find, Luther is dead and has been placed in front of us as a decoy. In the background we hear Toteras laughing as he says: "The mind-fuck is over. Those of you who can't understand, get the Hell out." Toteras does not stop with merely interchanging characters, he continues and interchanges the events, playing back the same event with different actors and a completely different structure. The trial of Picalo, the sadistic massacre of a pair of shoes, are retold again from the eyes of a complete imbecile in the confessions of Bambalamba, which becomes the most dramatic part of the play. Bambalamba witnesses the kangaroo court execution of Leo by

Big Fella; the confession becomes a ritual, Abraham offering his son for sacrifice to appease the vengeance of God, Picalo offered for sacrifice after being recreated again from the ashes of Leo to become, "The Patron Saint of Thieves and Murderers," the saint of the criminal.

The fatal gap that drama creates between the promise and the performance, between the desire and its projection, has always been filled with the role of the critic, the apologist, the advocators of the aesthetical contract between creaor and audience. Toteras destroys the attitude if not the concept. "The actors have come from within me to perform in a world that I have created for myself . . . . All through the affair the audience will always be ME and I shall let the actors know what I want as they continue."

The ontological problem posed to the Western mind, of the metaphysical man as apposed to the immediacy of the external man, becomes irrelevant to Toteras. He is all the actors. He is the valid and the invalid, the statement and the paradox. He is both sides of the coin, evoking for the audience a state of constant fluidity.

Though one might take the map as the territory, it is not—nor is the territory the description of the forces which gave it existence. The handy tools, the appropriate clichés, so beneficial for ingressing into the inner world, are outdated and for the lack of understanding and appropriate terminology, we often refer to it as incomprehensible, non-functional, deviate, or possibly even, sick. The recognizable, the familiar, becomes the comprehensible, interwined in stock situations and prearranged responses. The savage god of Yeats is the incomprehensible, the tormentor of dramatic convention. The metaphysical man of Artaud becomes the necessitator of new attitudes, attitudes that will permit us to become, even for a moment, voyagers within an inner world of dreams, sounds, emotions, which reason itself forbids us to ever see, hear or feel: a world where its creator makes no attempt to make the subjective into an objective world of general understanding.

SIX POEMS

QUINCY TROUPE

FOR WES, AN ELEGY

". . . and the fabric weakens"

Wes, you sat there,
sat there absorbing
all the beauty in the world
all the ugliness in the world
all the frustrations
in the world, sat there absorbing
all the imperfections, and perfections
of this imperfect world,
because you were Black, —and human!
like me, like 'Roi,
like the 'Trane, like the "Bird,"
sat there, playing beautiful sounds
of the streets of our ghettos,
because you knew the meaning
of the words
                    Love,
                              Brotherhood,
                                                  Fraternity,

knew the meaning well;
                                        i could hear it
when your music soared
and filled my heart with immortal joy;
wondrous sounds of euphonious harmony
weaved thru octavian chords,
speaking of "niggertown" heritage:
and the sometimes savage nights of "Naptown,"
sounds of fine sugar brown sisters
slidin' down music infested streets,
their hips playing rhythms on the wind,
sounds of brothers boppin',
sportin' heavy naturals;
hustlers, with straws cocked:
acey-deucey to the side,
sounds of people hummin',
cars blaring,
images of Hollywood,
sunset and vine, the "Whiskey
A Go-Go," New York's busy streets,
the subways, the taxis,
San Francisco and Fillmore Street,
photographic sounds etched on blue air,
filtering thru rum filled rooms
buoyant with Black tears
and Black laughter

Black sounds
Human sounds
Groovy sounds
cookin' from the rooms on my street
blues streets
Black streets
spinning from the jaws of jukeboxes,
swinging unforgettably thru the air,
your sounds, guitar sounds,
your thumb gliding deliberately,
lovingly over the strings,
sounds, weaving in and out of

octavian harmonies,
climbing the fabled stairs to where
Charlie left his "Solo Flight,"
and went off to pay his last dues

Wes, you sat there,
poised, on your stool,
absorbing all the things in this world,
and even in your sadness, in your pain,
in your quest for living perfection,
you gave us beauty,
you gave us joy, you gave us hope

We will miss you Wes,
we will miss you Wes.

EXQUISITE

Success!
The moment
of truth. . .
bringing a long
journey to an end:
now, to sleep.
Miles . . . searching,
haunting. . .
taking a woman
for myself, to love
and to cherish. . . . .
having children
search my face
for answers, thinking
in solitude
of money and fame,
seeing the reality
of those thoughts,

Paris France at midnight
when the breeze
from the river Seine
drifts beneath the bridges
causing lovers to shiver
with delight. . . . .
that which
my love means
to me
life.

FLIES ON SHIT

Mah man,
you ever watched
flies on shit?
Ah mean how they gather 'round
and hover hover over
and buzz and buzz and buzz
and then descend into the stink,
into the realness of that stink?!
Ah mean, mah man, have you ever
watched a fly eat shit
every day all day long
each and every day
flapping wings
but never ever
flying away for too long,
always coming back
to buzz and buzz and buzz
until the stink is there no longer
now an old turd
brick hard in the sun,
now crumbling crumbling
now falling away
to dust,

you know,
human folks are like that,
always in the shit,
but never ever
flying away.

A DAY IN THE LIFE OF A POET

Woke up crying the blues:
bore witness to the sadness of the day;
the peaceful man from Atlanta
was slaughtered yester/day.
Got myself together
drank in the sweetness of sunshine,
wrote three poems to the peaceful lamb
from Atlanta; made love
to a raging Black woman
drank wine
got high: saw angels
leading the lamb to heaven?
the blues gonna get me!
went to the beach to forget
about the gentle soul from Georgia;
ate clam chowder soup and fish sandwiches;
made love in the sand
to this same beautiful woman:
drank in all her sweetness:
saw the blood sun falling
behind weeping purple clouds;
tears fell in rivers for this gentle lamb
whom I cant forget.
The bloody star sinking
into the purple grave: blackness falls.
Go out into the decay of day;
'copped three keys';

the key of happiness,
the key of creative joy,
the key of sadness.
Came back and watched the gloom on the tube
at her house; which was disrupted.
Kissed her: went home by the route
of the mad freeways: dropped tears in my lap
for the lamb in Atlanta.
Home at last.
Two letters under the door;
a love letter from the past
grips at the roots of memory:
at last another poem published; good news
during a bad news weekend;
lights out;
drink of grapes;
severed sight
closes another day
in the life.

TO A CAT I KNOW

burning up the roads
with American bullshit
you go flipping and flying
spacing on dope
lapping up the wine
of decaying vineyards
waiting on hope.
will it ever come?
was it ever promised.

POEM FOR FRIENDS

1

the earth
is a wonderful
yet morbid place
filled with the complexities
of living
                    seeking death
we come to organs
which are shaped like wish bones,
forks that are roads
of indecision
                    and
we go with footsteps
that are either heavy
or light (depending
upon your weight,
your substance.

we go into
light or darkness (depending
upon the perception
of your vision.

we flounder
we climb, we trip
we fall, we call on
dead prophets to help us

                              yet
they do not answer us (we hear
instead
the singing in the leaves
the waves of the oceans pounding.

we see the sheer cliffs
of mountains polished by the storms;
sculptured to Allahs perfection.

we see the advancing age of technology;
of soul-less monsters
eating up nature's perfections

we hear wails and screams
                    and sirens howling

but we hear no human voices calling

we sit at the brink of chaos laughing,
we idle away time
when there is no time
left us

we jump out of airplanes
with no parachutes,
we praise the foul madmen
of war; we are pygmalions
in love with bleak stones:

and aphrodite is not here
                    to save us.
                    seeking death
we come to organs
which are shaped like wish bones,
forks that are roads
of indecision

                    and
we go with footsteps
that are either heavy
or light (depending
upon your weight
your substance, down unknown roads
seeking life in an ocean of darkness.

2

journey if you can
to the far poles of the world,
there you will find
flocks of sick birds
dying in the blue sea that is sky,
you will find
herds of dying animals
huddled together in the snow
'gainst the cold
but with no touch
of each other,
no knowledge of who they are,
no love for their space that breathes,
no love for what they can be
they gaze each day eagerly
into seas of light seeking darkness.

3

the mind is so wide
and wide again,
so broad and deep
and deep again

fardown we go
so slow into glow
and there find knowledge
of who we are

but go slow Effendi,
go slow from here
from everywhere,
go slow into sadness
of who we are,
go slow into slow dance
of what you are

go slow Effendi,
go slow into beauty
of space and time and distance,
measure every breath
that you breathe,
for it is precious,
it is holy

go free into sun-lit days,
fly free like the African ibis
confronting the wind,
swim long in the currents of these times
like the dolphin
plunging free through blue waves

and the faces that we see
upon the curl
of the foam
of the fingered blue waters
are the faces of the world:
the sandstones that are hourglasses
to be deposited upon our shores

they are new seeds
in need of nourishment
in search for love,
in need of beauty, requesting wisdom;
they are children of the universe,
glissando falling
upon our gold plated shores
that are reefs,
that are varicose veins;
peeping up
from the shallowness
of these red waters, savage rocks,
islands where all life
is banned

4

we must investigate our bodies,
we must investigate our sources of beauty,
we must investigate our images;
the parade of decayed heroes that we see,
that we help invent,
we must probe and descend into life-styles
like surgeons seeking cancer;
we must cut away
with truth's scalpel
all verbose flesh, all diseased portions;
we must fly free and weightless
like a summer breeze
to the nest of truth's sanctuary

5

the shell is bursting
from within
from without

in order to go out
we must come in
so come in, come in
go out, go out
            go out there now Effendi

to the places
where the good folks gather,
talk to everyone
for everyone is someone
whose life is important
to someone too everyone
whose flesh is a part of your own
universe
for the universe

is a continual cycle
from the sun to the clouds
to the rains feeding the earth
and the green of the forests
and the blue of the lakes
reflecting the brilliance of the sky
and the blood of the lions pouring
through the poems of mankind
and the "grass" lending depth
to our cosmorific visions
that are all,
                    i say all a part of you
a part of me
& we are but extensions
of this universe's magnificent workings,
but sandstones on the beaches of chaos,
but specks—not even stars!
on the vistas of darkness

so
come in, come in,
go out, go out,
be beautiful for all peoples of this world

walk free, walk proud, walk tall
Effendi,
walk back into the streets
free streets, that are ours

go now, go now,
go now Effendi,
do your thang,
the righteous thang,
your own thang
                    for the world
too save the world
too save the world
too save yourself.

SKULLSHAPES

CHARLES TOMLINSON

Skulls. Finalities. They emerge toward new beginnings from undergrowth. Along with stones, fossils, flint keel-scrapers and spokeshaves, along with bowls of clay pipes heel-stamped with their makers' marks, comes the rural detritus of cattle skulls brought home by children. They are moss-stained, filthy with soil. Washing them of their mottlings, the hand grows conscious of weight, weight sharp with jaggednesses. Suspend them from a nail and one feels the bone-clumsiness go out of them: there is weight still in their vertical pull downward from the nail, but there is also a hanging fragility. The two qualities fuse and the brush translates this fusion as wit, where leg-like appendages conclude the skulls' dangling mass.

Shadow explores them. It sockets the eye-holes with black. It reaches like fingers into the places one cannot see. Skulls are a keen instance of this duality of the visible: it borders what the eye cannot make out, it transcends itself with the suggestion of all that is there beside what lies within the eyes' possession: it cannot be possessed. Flooded with light, the skull is at once manifest surface and labyrinth of recesses. Shadow reaches down out of this world of helmeted cavities and declares it.

One sees. But not merely the passive mirrorings of the retinal mosaic—nor, like Ruskin's blind man struck suddenly by vision, without memory or conception. The senses, reminded by other seeings, bring to bear on the act of vision their pattern of images; they give point and place to an otherwise naked and homeless impression. It is the mind sees. But what it sees consists not solely of that by which it is confronted grasped in the light of that which it remembers. It sees possibility.

The skulls of birds, hard to the touch, are delicate to the eye. Egg-like in the round of the skull itself and as if the spherical shape were the result of an act like glass-blowing, they resist the eyes' imaginings with the blade of the beak, which no lyrical admiration can attenuate to frailty.

The skull of nature is recess and volume. The skull of art—of possibility—is recess, volume, and also lines—lines of containment, lines of extension. In seeing, one already extends the retinal impression, searchingly and instantaneously. Brush and pen extend the search beyond the instant, touch discloses a future. Volume, knived across by the challenge of a line, the raggedness of flaking bone countered by ruled, triangular facets, a cowskull opens a visionary field, a play of universals.

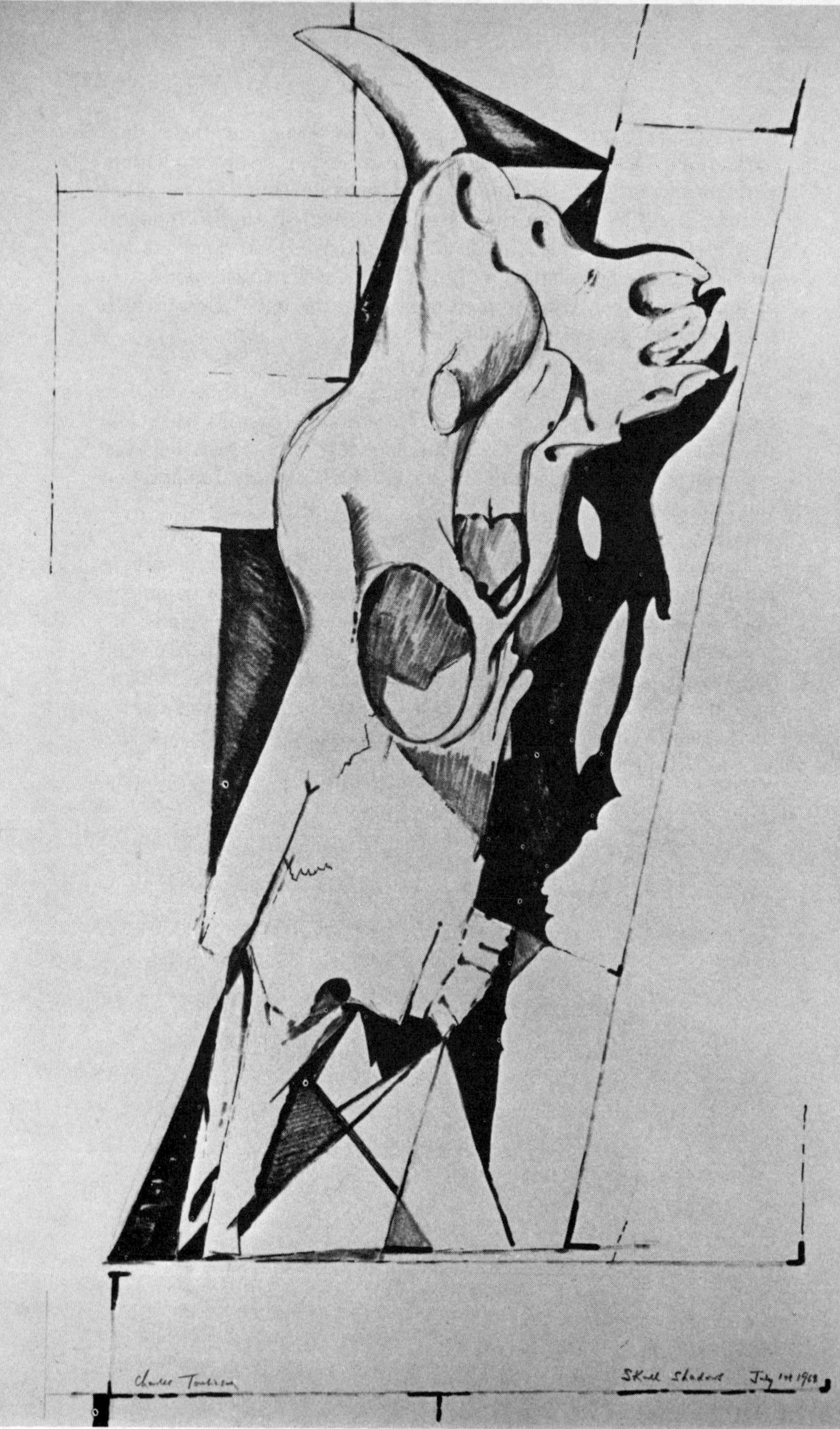
Charles Tomlinson
Skull Shadows

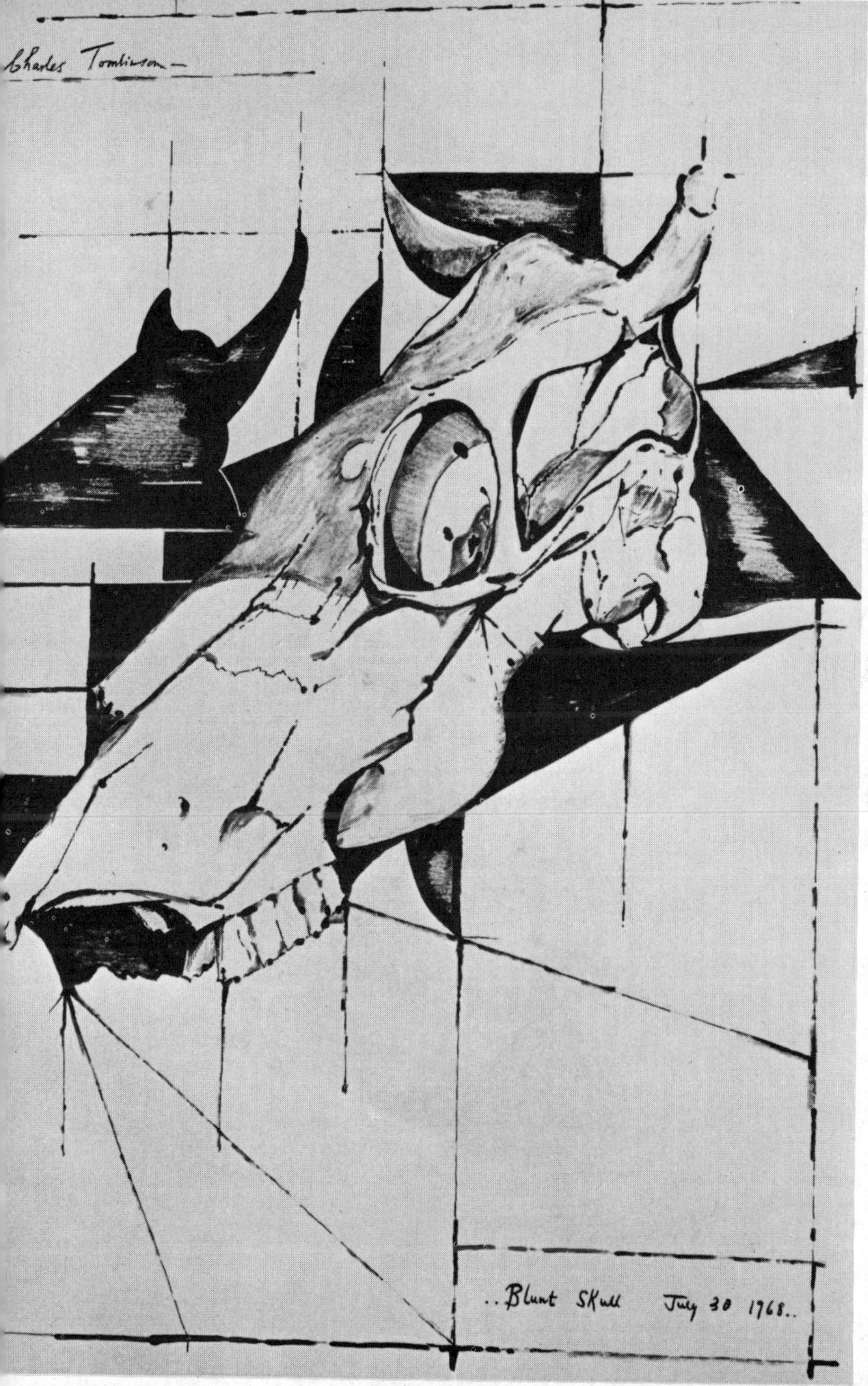
Charles Tomlinson—
..Blunt Skull July 30 1968..

Charles Tomlinson Oct 4 1968

Seagull Skull.

Horizontal Skull August 4th 1968
Charles Tomlinson

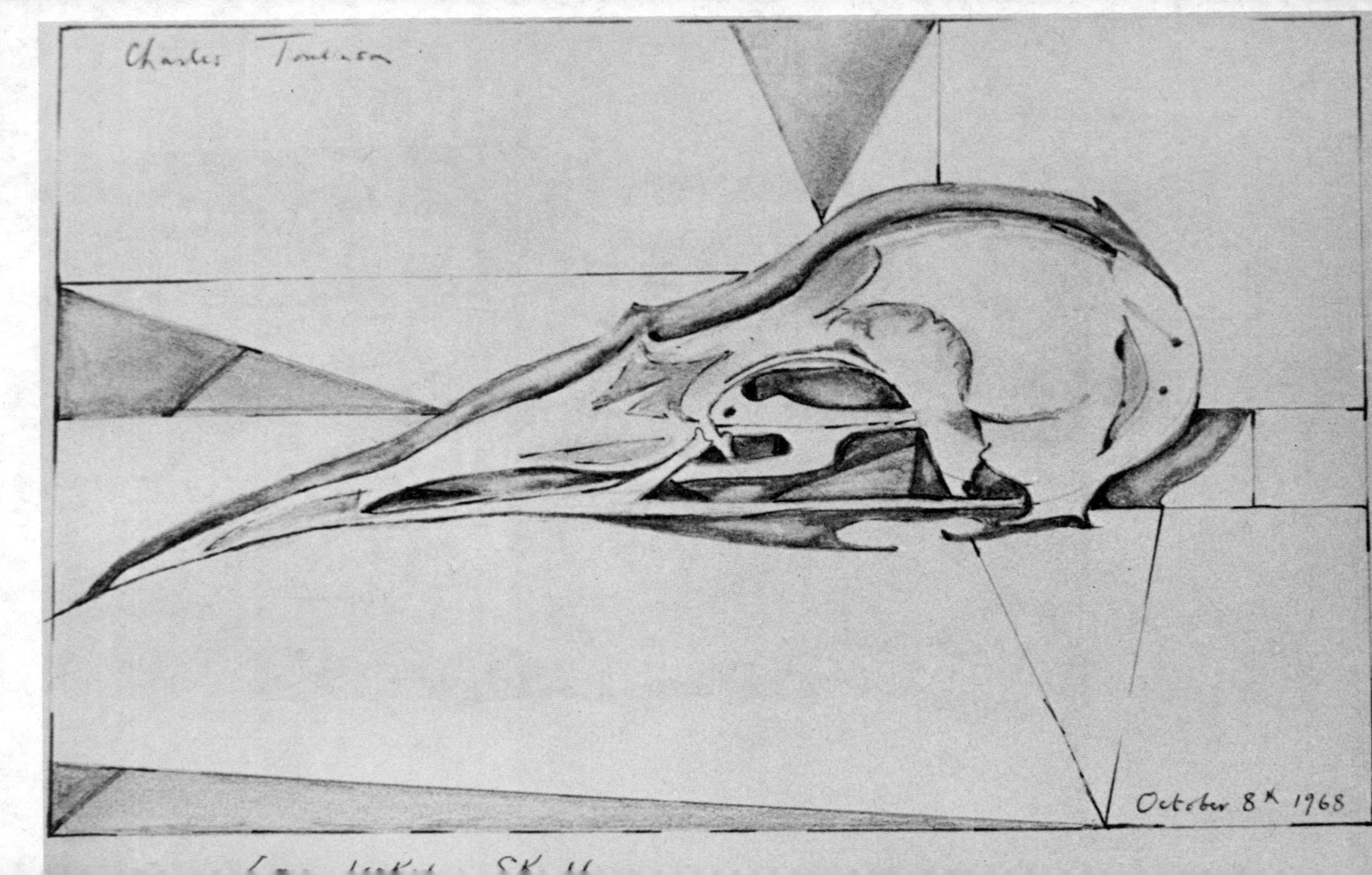
October 8 X 1968

MY FATHER'S GOLDEN DREAM

ROBERT LOWRY

One night in Greenwich Village
in the pad on Bleecker Street where I was living
my father came back to me in a dream three years after
his death (though he was as real as you or I
standing there) and told me—he told me
that he would now give me my instructions
for the creation of his monument:
"From the moment of my birth on January the Eighteenth, 1886,"
he said,
"to the moment of my death on the midnight commencing
August First, 1958," he said,
"put it all in gold," he said.
"In gold, Dad?" I said.
"Put those years in gold, Bob," he said.
"You mean the rivers actually running as liquid gold, Dad?"
I asked. "The rivers," he replied,
"running as liquid gold, Bob."
"And the people—"
"Make them gold people, with gold organs."
"But the contrasts," I said.
"Make them," he said, "contrasts of different shades
of gold. Reddish gold for red hair. White gold
for white skin. Browner gold for brown eyes."
"I'll need a lot of help, Dad,

to put a whole era in gold, and all
just as it was."
"Let everyone work on it," Dad said, "even babies
are welcome. And let it all be perfect."
"What can babies do, Dad?" I asked. "They can
work on the raindrops of all the rains that fell
during my day," Dad said. "And if every raindrop
is not perfect and just as it was when it fell,
babies can be forgiven. But let the rest be perfect
and just as it was
except that it will be in gold."

NOTES ON CONTRIBUTORS

The poet, playwright and essayist GOTTFRIED BENN (1886-1956) occupies a position in modern German literature which is perhaps comparable to that of Pound and Eliot in English. His experiments with the language and forms of verse, and his exploration of whole new areas of subject matter, did for German poetry what the Expressionists did for painting. *The Voice behind the Curtain* (*Die Stimme hinter dem Vorhang*) was first published in 1951. A volume of selected writings of Benn, in translation, *Primal Vision*, is in print on the New Directions list. DAVID HARRIS, translator of *The Voice behind the Curtain*, is an American living in Germany, where he is completing his doctoral thesis at the Free University of West Berlin.

PAUL BRESLOW is a journalist, critic and fiction writer who lives in New York City. He has done political essays for the English quarterly *Twentieth Century*, film reviews for *Vogue*, and book reviews for *The Nation*, *Commentary* and *Dissent*. Two of his stories have appeared in *Transatlantic Review* and he is working on a novel.

CAROL EMSHWILLER lives in Wantagh on Long Island. She is married to an experimental filmmaker; they have three children. Her stories have been published in *Transatlantic Review*, *Epoch*, *New Worlds* (England) and *Fantasy and Science Fiction*.

LAWRENCE FERLINGHETTI's most recent books on the New Directions list are *Tyrannus Nix?*, a political tirade, and *The Secret Meaning of Things*, a collection of poems, which includes "Assassination Raga," on the death of Robert Kennedy. In 1968 Ferlinghetti was awarded one of the most important European literary prizes, the Premio Internazionale di Poesie Etna-Taormina.

The Scottish poet IAN HAMILTON FINLAY is, as Jonathan Williams has put it, a *maker:* of poems, plays, ponds, gardens and boats. Though he is known as the leading concrete poet writing in English, he "dislikes experiment, whether on poetry or animals." His poems, which may be realized on the page or in such materials as stone or sandblasted glass, often deal with fishingboats and the sea. Finlay's concrete poems are included in the Something Else Press *Anthology of Concrete Poetry* and in J-F. Bory's *Once Again* (New Directions). His earlier sequence of poems *The Dancers Inherit the Party* is available here in the *New Directions 20* anthology.

PAUL FRIEDMAN lives in Urbana, Illinois, with his wife and daughter. His "Portrait: My American Man, Fall, 1966" was in *ND20* and he has also published stories in *North American Review*, *Perspective*, *Quarterly Review of Literature* and *Trace*.

JAMES B. HALL is Provost of "College Five" on the University of California, Santa Cruz campus. New Directions published his book of stories, *Us He Devours*, in 1964, and he was one of the three writers in the ND anthology *15 x 3* in 1957. Among his other books are three novels: *Not by the door* (1954), *Racers to the Sun* (1960) and *Mayo Sergeant* (1967).

ROBERT LOWRY, novelist and editor, lives in Cincinnati. As a young man, he founded The Little Man Press, and later he was on the staff of New Directions. ND published his war novel *Casualty* in 1947. Among his more recent books are *The Prince of Pride Starring* and *Party of Dreamers.*

RICHARD MEYERS was born in Kentucky, some twenty years ago, and grew up there. He dropped out of high school to come to New York to write. With David Giannini, he is co-editor of the magazine *Genesis:Grasp.*

MARK JAY MIRSKY was born in 1939 in Boston, where his father was a lawyer and politician in the 14th Ward. After Boston Public Latin School, he went to Harvard, then took an M.A. at Stanford. He later taught at Stanford in John Hawkes' "Voice Project," and he is now directing a similar program in composition at City College of New York. His first novel, *Thou Worm Jacob,* was published by Macmillan in 1967, and a section from his second novel, still unpublished as a whole, is included in Jerome Charyn's anthology *The Single Voice.*

STUART MONTGOMERY is editor and publisher of Fulcrum Press in London. He has brought the work of many American poets, among them, Robert Duncan, Gary Snyder, Charles Olson and George Oppen, to English readers.

VASKO POPA was born in Grebenac, in the Banat region of Yugoslavia, in 1922. A graduate of the University of Belgrade, he has published three books of poems: *Kora* (*Bark*) in 1953, *Nepočin-Polje* (*A Field without Beginning*) in 1956 and *Sporedno Nebo* (*The Secondary Sky*) in 1968. Penguin Books brought out a *Selected Poems* in translation in 1969. The poems printed here are from the revised edition of *Kora* (1969). STEPHEN STEPANCHEV, the translator, was born in Yugoslavia in 1915 and came to this country at the age of seven. He is a Professor of English at Queens College in Flushing. He has published three books of poetry: *Three Priests in April* (1956), *Spring in the Harbor* (1967), *A Man Running in the Rain* (1969) and a critical survey, *American Poetry since 1945* (1965).

A first book of poems by ED ROBERSON, *When Thy King Is a Boy*, will be published by University of Pittsburgh Press next month. He was born in Pittsburgh in 1939, worked there for a time as a zookeeper and is now on the faculty of the University.

DENNIS SILK, a British journalist, has been living in Jerusalem since 1955 and has served in the Israeli army. "Montefiore" is from a sequence of fantastic stories about journeys to Jerusalem, Malta and the Dead Sea; "Tryphon," first in the sequence, appeared in *Encounter*. He has also published a book of poems, *A Face of Stone*, several puppet-plays and *Retrievements: A Jerusalem Anthology* (Israel Universities Press).

RYUICHI TAMURA, born in 1923, was raised in Otsuka, a section of Tokyo which was an old Geisha district, still almost a feudalistic world. His sensibilities have remained traditional Japanese but he has been influenced by Western poetry in English, translated Eliot's *Waste Land* and was a founder-editor of the influential literary magaine *Arechi* ("The Waste Land") after World War II. His books are: *Four Thousand Days and Nights* (1956), *The World without Words* (1962), *A Study of Fear* (1966) and *A Green Thought* (1967). The translators are SAMUEL GROLMES, an American poet and Fulbright Fellow, now teaching at Tezukayama Gakuin University in Osaka, and his wife, YUMIKO TSUMURA.

The English poet and critic CHARLES TOMLINSON, who lives in Gloucestershire and lectures at Bristol University, is a leading authority in England on modern American poetry. He has held visiting professorships in this country at the University of New Mexico and Colgate. His books of poetry include *The Necklace, Seeing is Believing, A Peopled Landscape* and *American Scenes,* and, in collaboration with Henry Gifford, he has published volumes of translations of Tyutchev and Machado.

DEMETRIUS TOTERAS is an American now living on one of the Greek islands. He enlisted, with altered documents, in the US army at the age of fifteen, served in Korea and spent eighteen months as a prisoner of war. He has also done time in civil prisons, the background for "Sunday They'll Make Me a Saint" and much of his other writing. A film of "Sunday," produced by George Brandt and James Katsaros at Bristol University in England, has been shown at the Edinburgh, Amsterdam and Berlin Film Festivals. JAMES POTTS, whose essay on Toteras follows the scene from the play, is a British freelance film director and literary critic. He has made eight films and did the shooting script for "Sunday They'll Make Me a Saint."

QUINCY TROUPE was born in New York City in 1943, grew up in St. Louis, then attended Grambling College in Louisiana on a basketball scholarship. He went into the army and visited fourteen foreign countries. In Paris, he met Sartre and Chester Himes, and was inspired by them to become a writer. Later he joined Budd Schulberg's Writers' Workshop in Watts and there edited the *Watts Poets & Writers* anthology. He has been managing editor of the magazine *Shrewd* in Los Angeles, is an activist in the Black Revolution and has given poetry readings all over the country.

Last year AL YOUNG won the Joseph Henry Jackson Award for poetry in San Francisco and he is now Jones Lecturer in Creative Writing at Stanford University. He was born in Mississippi in 1940, grew up there and in Detroit, attended the University of Michigan, wandered the country "working & scuffling," visited Europe, then settled in the Bay Area. His first collection of poems, *Dancing,* was recently published by Corinth Books, New York, and "For Poets" has been chosen for the third annual *American Literary Anthology.* He is now teaching at Ohio University in Athens, Ohio.